Coping Strategies for Living Abroad

A Self-assessment Workbook to Reduce Stress and Live the Life You Want

by James E. McGinley, PhD

Copyright © 2020 by James E. McGinley

Contents

Supplemental material

Profiles

Meet Matt	(digital nomad)
Meet Mike	(semi-retired)
Meet Tal	(spouse)
Meet Max	(corporate worker)
Meet Alexa	(TEFL worker)
Meet Jim and Jiab	(retiree)

Spotlight on culture

Greetings
Time
Personal space
Handling conflict
Respect for elders

Worksheets

Exercise #1: Who am I?

Exercise #2: What kind of expatriate am I?

Exercise #3: What is important to me?

Exercise #4: Culture shock inventory

Exercise #5: Where am I on the adjustment curve?

Exercise #6: How do I describe myself?

Exercise #7: My groups

Exercise #8: My strengths

Exercise #9: How I cope

Exercise #10: My goals

Exercise #11: Self-assessment

Exercise #12: My learning styles

Exercise #13: My social connections

Exercise #14: Challenging negative thoughts

Exercise #15: Alternative thinking

Exercise #16: Solving problems

Exercise #17: Simple meditation

Exercise #18: Visualizing success

Exercise #19: My legacy

Exercise #20: A hero's/heroine's journey

INTRODUCTION

Living abroad can be exciting and rewarding, but it also can be frustrating and stressful. Much of the difficulty with living abroad is based on how well we cope with living in a different cultural environment. This book examines cultural adjustment, gives you some opportunities for self-assessment, and provides a few simple, manageable coping strategies to help you successfully adjust while living abroad.

THE EXPATRIATE

The term expatriate is derived from the Latin 'ex' (out of) and 'patria' (country). It can be a noun or a verb. As a noun, it means one who lives outside their native country as in: "A Canadian expatriate living in Japan." As a verb, it means to live or settle abroad as in, "This job requires you to expatriate to Russia."

What is an expatriate?

An expatriate is someone who lives outside his or her native country. Two common differences among expatriates are the length of time they have spent abroad and their intention to return home. Some expatriates have left their home country only temporarily, some permanently, and some have left for an indeterminate amount of time. Common temporary expatriates include long-stay tourists and workers. Some expatriates have decided to leave their home country permanently, for example retirees or persons who have changed their citizenship. Many people who live abroad have not made a final decision on when they will return home. To them, not having a schedule is part of the meaning and fun of being an expatriate. They enjoy having the freedom to live life freely and explore the world without firm commitments.

Expat Insider is one of the world's largest and most comprehensive surveys of life abroad. In 2019 it surveyed 20,259 expatriates from around the world who represented 182 nationalities and are scattered across 187 countries or territories. The survey found that 31 percent of expatriates planned to live abroad for less than 5 years, 19 percent for longer than 5 years, 32 percent reported possibly living abroad forever, and 18 percent were undecided about their planned length of stay

The term expatriate commonly refers to persons who live abroad for an extended period of time and have undergone some degree of acculturation within the host country. They have learned the nuances of daily life in another country, have learned to navigate its immigration system, and have an insider's perspective on its people and culture. To many people, being an expatriate is both a mindset and a lifestyle.

> *Being an expat is a lifestyle choice and goes way beyond what a tourist would experience. It's a huge difference, which is why tourists and expats often have totally different mindsets.*
>
> *Wendy*

Expatriate demographics
The Expat Insider's 2019 survey indicated that the gender of expatriates worldwide was evenly split between men (49%) and women (51%). The majority of expatriates (63%) reported being in a relationship versus being single (37%). However, 79 percent reported living abroad without dependent children, while 21 percent reported living with dependent children. The average age of expatriates was 44 years old, with the following distribution: 25 years old and below (4%), 26-30 years old (12%), 31-35 years old (15%), 36-40 years old (14%), 41-50 years old (23%), and 51 years old and above (32%).

How many expatriates are there?
There is no definitive count of the number of expatriates worldwide. This is understandable since there are many types of expatriates and there is no mechanism to count or keep track of them. Here are a few expatriate counts that give us some insight into the scope of the world's expatriate population.

By their nature, universities are global organizations. It was estimated that in 2017, there were over 5.3 million international students worldwide, up from 2 million in 2000.

The U.S. Department of State only occasionally releases statistical estimates on expatriates. Its last data release in 2016 indicated that there were 9 million U.S. citizens living abroad. In 2016, there were 70,666 registered births of U.S. citizens abroad and 10,992 U.S. expatriates passed away while overseas.

The European Union estimates that 2.4 million migrants entered the European Union in 2018. As of 1 January 2019, 21.8 million (4.9%) of the 446.8 million persons living in European Union countries were not European Union citizens.

The United Nations estimated that the number of international migrants worldwide reached 272 million persons in 2019. This is an increase of 51 million since 2010. The United Nations estimates that international migrants comprise 3.5 percent of the world's population, compared to 2.8 percent in the year 2000.

Why do people live abroad?

The technical definition of an expatriate is straightforward, but it does not capture the full picture. What motivates a person to live abroad? How do they see themselves? How do they see living abroad as a lifestyle?

There is an incredible variety of persons who live abroad, either by choice or by circumstance. These persons include tourists, sojourners, international students, international business people, retirees, immigrants, and refugees. This variety makes it difficult to summarize expatriates. However, many people live abroad for a purpose, such as work, travel, romance, or retirement.

Primary motivations

The Expat Insider's 2019 survey found that the primary motivations for living abroad included work, lifestyle choices, education, love, and family. Work included job and career factors such as finding a job in the country on their own (14%), being send abroad by an employer (10%), being recruited internationally (9%), and a desire to start their own business (3%). Lifestyle factors included seeking a better quality of life (9%), looking for adventure or a personal change (6%), financial reasons (3%), to live in a particular country or city (3%), and to simply enjoy living abroad (3%).

Education factors included to go to school or university (6%) and to improve language skills (1%). Love and family factors included to live in a partner's home country or for love (12%), for a partner's job or education (7%), or other family reasons (5%). Other reasons for living abroad included other (4%), political, religious, or safety reasons (2%), and volunteering or missionary work (1%).

Digital Nomads

The internet has globally connected the world, opening up new opportunities to combine work, travel, and leisure into a new lifestyle. People who take advantage of this opportunity are called digital nomads. The idea extends beyond being a global teleworker. Digital nomads travel freely. They use the internet to generate income. They tend to embrace an alternative lifestyle that values personal freedom, enjoyment of life, and creativity. It is not surprising that many are bloggers, writers, photographers, and internet marketeers. But others are project managers, IT specialists, and teachers. Independent-minded workers have often chosen to work the way they do for personal reasons such as work-life balance, flexibility, and control - a lifestyle that is supported by being a digital nomad.

Meet Matt

Matt is one of about 5 million people who describe themselves as digital nomads, although as many as 17 million people aspire to be digital nomads. While most will not make the transition, many enjoy watching and following the travels of nomads like Matt. Matt's lifestyle matched the popular image of the digital nomad as an internet-based freelancer who constantly traveled from place to place.

Matt decided to become a blogger, to save money he sold all his belongings and began backpacking around the world blogging about his travels. He built a successful business and spent 7 years traveling almost non-stop. He visited over 50 countries, living for months at a time in places like Thailand, Mexico, Turkey, Spain, Nicaragua, and South Africa. Everything he owned fit into two backpacks.

Matt's aspirations changed as he began to tire of constant travel, developed an urge to return to home in the United States, and became weary of the struggles that are a part of a nomadic lifestyle. He still generates income from the internet and travels, just from a more permanent base now. He has developed a new philosophy of what it means to be location independent.

I wouldn't trade the last 7 years of my life working as a traveling digital nomad for anything else. It's been a wild ride, and the experience has taught me so much about myself and the world in general.

Matt

Exercise #1
Who am I?

(Who we are today is shaped, in part, by our past experiences, good and bad, how we look at them, and how we use them to define ourselves.)

Respond to the following questions:

My triumphs and challenges:

1. What are some of the proudest moments of your life? What kinds of trying and stressful experiences have you survived in which you felt more powerful and capable of meeting challenges?

____

____

____

____

____

2. How have successes and triumphs shaped your life? How have they changed the way in which you view yourself, your goals, your dreams?

____

____

____

____

____

Who do I want to become?

1. Describe the kind of person that you want to become.

____

____

____

____

____

____

2. What would you most like to change about yourself? What do you want your life to be like in five years?

____

____

____

____

____

____

Exercise #2:

What kind of expatriate am I?

(There are many different kinds of expatriates. Moving abroad is often shaped by our reasons for moving and our future intentions to move again or to return home.)

Respond to the following questions:

Why did I move abroad? What were my goals? What do I want?

____

____

____

____

____

____

How long do I plan to live abroad?

____

____

____

____

____

How will I know when it is time for me to move again or return home? How will I know when I will never move again?

____

____

____

____

____

CULTURE

Culture is everywhere around us. It shapes how we think, what we believe, what we value, and how we interact with one another. A key feature of living abroad is the fact that we are immersed in another culture, although we bring our own culture with us. This cross-cultural contact often highlights the differences between people.

What is culture?

Culture is the total collective of how a society thinks and behaves. It includes dress, language, rituals, norms of behavior, and systems of beliefs, including symbols and the importance we attach to them. Culture is so far reaching that is difficult to imagine any aspect of life that is not shaped by it. From birth to death, we are immersed in culture.

Formally, culture is the customary beliefs, social forms, and material traits of a racial, religious, or social group. A sociologist understands culture as the languages, customs, beliefs, rules, arts, knowledge, and collective identities and memories developed by members of all social groups that make their social environments meaningful.

Culture includes the following:
- How we dress and live
- How we talk to and interact with one another
- Our sense of what is right and what is wrong
- How we structure the world around us
- Our beliefs and values
- Our sense of self-worth and how we value others
- Important signs and symbols
- The social rules and rituals we observe as we go through life.

Culture has an immense scale. It is both broad and intimate. Things that may seem to be parts of our natural lives, e.g., birth, sexuality, aging, death, are all shaped and given meaning by culture. Even behaviors as simple as greeting someone or eating a meal are given meaning by culture and shaped by accepted customs and practices.

Culture is expressed in an unlimited number of ways. The diversity of culture is part of why it is fun and exciting. Everyone loves new and different things. There is nothing we have experienced that cannot be re-experienced in a new and different way in another culture. Part of the fun of cultural diversity also comes from the mixing of cultures together. Holidays are typically rich in symbols and traditions. If you have experienced a holiday season abroad, you have probably seen the mixing of different holidays and holiday traditions together as your traditions and the traditions of the host country merge.

Culture is both external and internal. Culture shapes how we interpret the world and how we feel. It influences our views, values, sense of humor, loyalties, hopes, aspirations, and our worries and fears. Culture teaches us patterns of behavior that we have unconsciously adopted, but it also teaches us unconscious patterns of how we think and we emotionally react.

Culture anchors our personal identity and shapes how we see ourselves and others. Imagine in your mind a student or a farmer. What images does it bring? Now consider how someone in Asia, Europe, Latin America, or the Middle East would imagine them. Each image will be shaped by the culture that each person has been raised in, so they will likely be different. Beyond the image, culture also shapes our expectations of how we believe students and farmers should act. We can turn this lens on ourselves as well. Whatever role we have in life, such as friend, parent, student, teacher, worker, boss, son, daughter, etc., we have learned through our culture. How we express ourselves, whether through language, writing, art, dancing, music, or sports, has been influenced by culture as well.

A very useful aspect of culture is that it is learned. Anything that can be learned, can be re-learned, modified, and adapted. So, culture has an inherent flexibility and adaptability. Geert Hofstede, a Dutch social scientist, defines culture as the collective programming of the mind that distinguishes the members of one group or category of people from others. A mind that can be programmed can be reprogrammed. There is probably no greater source of new inputs to reprogramming our minds than being exposed to a different culture.

> *Knowing and understanding the culture of a different country is not an overwhelming task, but it isn't something to take lightly.*
>
> *Vineeta*

What happens when cultures meet?

What happens when cultures meet depends on their differences and the circumstances they meet under.

Differences are important

Cross-cultural contact is shaped, in part, by how different cultures are from one another. Some cultures share many similarities and some do not.

Cultural distance

The term cultural distance refers to the similarities and differences between cultures. Dissimilar cultures are more culturally distant. Researchers have examined whether cultural distance impacts on cross-cultural adjustment. They have found that greater cultural distance is associated with adjustment stress and anxiety. Greater cultural distance means that expatriates are likely to experience more intense life changes during their cultural adjustment.

Cultural dimensions
Geert Hofstede, originally proposed that there were five dimensions of culture: individualism-collectivism, uncertainty avoidance, power distance (the strength of the social hierarchy), masculinity-femininity (task-orientation vs. person-orientation), and long-term orientation. Hofstede later added a sixth dimension (indulgence). These cultural dimensions can be measured to capture some of the similarities and differences between cultures.

United States and Thailand
When Hofstede's cultural dimensions are used to compare the United States and Thailand, the results highlight some of their cultural differences. For example, the United States has high score for individualism (91/100) and a fairly low score for power distance (40/100). On the other hand, Thailand has a low score for individualism (20/100) and a fairly high score for power distance (64/100).

Differences in individualism reflect a society's orientation towards favoring an "I" versus a "We" self-image. The United States has one of the highest scores in the world for individualism, so its culture favors an "I" self-image that emphasizes a high degree of personal independence. This may manifest as people feeling a responsibility to look after themselves and direct family members only. Thailand favors a "We" self-image. It emphasizes a high degree of personal interdependence. This may manifest as people feeling a responsibility to look after direct and extended family as well as other extended relationships in society.

Differences in power distance reflect the degree to which a society is comfortable with conditions in which society expects and accepts that power is not distributed equally. The United States has a fairly low power distance score, indicating that its society favors individual rights and opportunities to access power. Thailand has a fairly high score for power distance, indicating that society is more accepting of a power hierarchy where roles and rules are more clearly defined and accepted, even when some inequalities may exist.

> *When you travel, remember that a foreign country is not designed to make you comfortable. It is designed to make its own people comfortable.*
>
> *Clifton*

Thailand and South Korea

The United States and Thailand have very different measures for individualism and power distance. However, when Thailand is compared to South Korea, a regional neighbor, the differences become similarities. Thailand's and South Korea's scores for individualism are both low at 20/100 and 18/100 respectively. This is a difference of only 2 points, compared to the difference between Thailand and the United States of 71 points. Thailand's and South Korea's scores for power distance are 64 and 60 respectively, a difference of 4 points. This compares to a difference of 24 points between Thailand and the United States.

The similarities between Thailand and South Korea indicate that cross-cultural contact will likely be easier since the societies share perspectives and preferences. Similar cultures tend to have similar values and rules of behavior. So, while individual practices and customs may vary, people will find that they are in a comfortably familiar society. This means that many of the unconscious rules they have learned in life will be more likely to work in the new culture.

They will likely feel more comfortable and less threatened by what is happening around them. The new culture will simply be easier to understand, consciously and unconsciously. While some internal cultural rules will need to modified, there will be fewer new rules to learn.

Traditional and secular societies

The World Values Survey was a global survey that assessed cultural opinions in more than 60 countries. The survey indicated that traditional and secular values were a major dimension of cultural variation. Traditional societies tended to emphasize the importance of religion, parent-child ties, deference to authority, and traditional family values. People who embraced these values also tended to reject divorce. Secular societies had opposite preferences than traditional societies. Secular societies placed less emphasis on religion, traditional family values, and authority. Divorce was seen as relatively acceptable. Islamic societies were asserted to be more strongly traditional. Asian societies occupied the middle zone, bridging traditional and secular values but trended more strongly towards the traditional. Western European societies were shown to be more secular.

Geographic proximity

Cultures from the same region are also more likely to have had cross-cultural contact before. So, each culture likely already has a knowledgeable understanding of one another. In a sense, geographic proximity can lead to cultural proximity. Cross-cultural contact could have a long historical record, some history and customs may even be shared. Yet, even when cultures are geographically close but culturally distant, it is likely that each society has a frame of reference already established by which they view and understand their regional neighbors. They are aware of their neighbors, their differences, and already have a mental model for understanding them.

Circumstances shape cultural encounters

Cross-cultural encounters are shaped by the circumstances that surround them. These circumstances may relate to the purpose, timespan, and location of the encounter and the degree to which the encounter seen as intimate and friendly or not.

A stereotypical short- or long-stay tourist may have a carefully bounded cross-cultural encounter. Their stay may be for a specified amount of time and may focus on experiencing selected resorts, attractions, and activities. They may predominantly experience the local culture through guided activities or by visiting maintained attractions. The services they receive may cater to their home country cultural preferences by providing familiar choices for food and accommodations along with local options. Tourists are exposed to culture but tend to be insulated from the need to make dramatic adjustments to it.

Long-term expatriates can stay in a country for many years, perhaps permanently. Rather than focusing on short-term activities, they may view living abroad as a lifestyle choice. There can be different factors for their choice to live abroad. Some may be attracted by a particular aspect of the host country and are drawn to it. Others may be dissatisfied with their home country and be relocating as an escape or to find an alternative. For some people, it may be a combination of both factors.

Long-term expatriates live within the society and economy of the host country, so they have to learn the art of daily living. This means they must learn and adapt to the formal laws and regulations of the host country as well as its informal customs and practices. Long-term expatriates tend to have a deeper understanding of the country and its people. Because they are immersed in the local culture and in daily life, they also have more exposure to, and a deeper understanding of, the problems and frustrations of living in the host country.

Researchers have proposed that cross-cultural contact makes people more aware and understanding of other cultures. So, we would expect some cross-cultural benefit from any cultural encounter, either short or long. However, studies have found that this is not necessarily true. Research has found that cross-cultural contact alone is not sufficient to create cultural acceptance. Cross-cultural contact can actually reinforce existing biases and prejudices.

Cross-cultural contact can lead to a variety of good and bad outcomes, including acculturation, synthesis, integration, assimilation, vacillation between the two cultures, self-segregation, and hostility. The key is the nature of the contact. Cross-cultural encounters tend to create better outcomes when the contact is positive, shares a common purpose, is not exploitive, is mutually beneficial, is less formal, is not distant, is more personal and intimate, and when it occurs within a broader and supportive social environment or context.

Cross-cultural outcomes

Major potential outcomes for cross-cultural contact include rejection, segregation, assimilation, and integration.

Rejection

In a cross-cultural encounter one or both cultures may simply reject the other. Cultural rejection is a two-way street. The foreigner may be rejected by members of the host country, or the foreigner may reject the host country culture. We should remember that when we are immersed in a new culture, we lose our familiar points of reference, even those that establish our identity. This explains why some people feel a loss of identity and a sense of detachment or social vertigo when they move abroad. This is a basic threat to our sense of self, so it is understandable that as a defense mechanism a person might reject the host country culture as a way to preserve their own sense of identity. The same perception of threat may be felt by members of the host country. They may feel that their sense of personal or group identity is threatened by the expatriate's culture and similarly reject the external culture as a defense mechanism.

Cultural rejection does not have to be permanent. In the process of cross-cultural adjustment, it is common for people to go through a period of frustration in which they reject aspects of the local culture and emotionally or physically withdraw in an effort to prevent being overwhelmed. This period of rejection and withdrawal is often simply a stepping stone in the cultural adjustment process and is typically followed by a period of acceptance and improved adjustment.

We tend to think of cross-cultural contact as occurring between the expatriate and the host nation. However, the expatriate community is not homogenous and often contains a variety of different sub-groups. Since the expatriate community is itself diverse and can include foreigners from many different countries, it raises the possibility for exclusion and discrimination from both the host nation and from other expatriates. One study found that, while half (52%) of expatriates reported that no one within the expatriate community would discriminate against them, a full one-third (34%) of expatriates reported that they believed that others within the expatriate community would discriminate. This perception is similar to perceived discrimination from the host nation. In the same study, one-third (36%) of expatriates reported someone from the host nation would discriminate against them.

Segregation

In a cross-cultural encounter the foreigner may self-segregate from the host country by limiting contact and exposure to locals or local culture. It has been observed that some tourists and expatriates live in a social or functional bubble where they can limit and control their degree of cultural exposure. To be fair, some expatriates do live in assigned housing in expatriate enclaves set up by the host-country or their corporate employer for matters of convenience and security. However, some expatriates may make a personal decision to limit their contact with locals to the necessary activities of daily life and may favor socializing with other expatriates, especially those who are from their country of origin or who speak their language.

There are inherent barriers to fully becoming a part of a different culture, so some degree of differentiation or separation is natural. Unless one is a native, it is probably not realistic to expect to be accepted as a local, even though one's level of acculturation is high. Seeking friendship with similar or like-minded people facing the same challenges is natural. The problem with self-segregation is that it can become a withdrawal behavior. When one purposefully withdraws from cultural interaction, they are committing a physical, social, and emotional act. It is not a surprise that studies have associated social withdrawal in expatriates with poorer cross-cultural adjustment.

Assimilation

Cultural assimilation is the process where a person completely modifies their culture to fit wholescale into the host nation culture. The term has met with increasing disapproval since it is associated with the host nation culture not being accepting of other cultures and is associated with forcing people to abandon their native cultures. Yet, assimilation is a possible outcome and some people do make a decision to shift their cultural identification or citizenship after exposure to a different culture that they are attracted to and strongly identify with.

Integration

Cultural integration allows cultures that meet to retain their core cultural identities, e.g., values, beliefs, and preferences, while cooperatively merging with each other to create a new shared experience. Integration allows is to retain our identities while finding new ways to live together and value each other. Integration focuses on enriching our lives through cross-cultural contact.

The term acculturation is sometimes used as well and has a similar meaning to integration. Like integration, acculturation is the process by which cross-cultural contact leads to the acquisition of new cultural patterns by one or both groups by adopting parts of the other culture. Acculturation is often used to describe generational effects as culture is transmitted between the host nation and follow-on immigrant generations (i.e., children, grandchildren). The terms enculturation and socialization are used as well.

Japan

In Japan, people greet each other by bowing. Most Japanese do not expect foreigners to know proper bowing rules, so a nod of the head is usually acceptable. Although shaking hands is uncommon, exceptions are made, especially in international business meetings. At formal meetings, business cards are exchanged during the introductions and there is a customary etiquette for how they are exchanged.

Russia

A firm, often very firm, handshake is a typical greeting when meeting someone in Russia. Russians also maintain direct eye contact while giving the appropriate greeting for the time of day. When meeting a Russian for the first time, male or female, shake hands firmly while retaining eye contact. Looking away can be considered rude and indifferent. Men should wait for a woman to offer her hand first. Russians also commonly introduce each other through a third person rather than directly introducing themselves. As a non-native, do not assume familiarity but wait and follow the lead of your Russian friends.

Saudi Arabia

Men who are meeting for the first time or know each other casually will shake hands. Men who are close friends or family may also add a kiss on each cheek. Men who are very close and loyal friends may greet one another by touching noses. Women friends hug and kiss when greeting. Contact between genders is discouraged. Men and women do not greet each other in public. Even in business situations, women should not extend their hand to be shaken.

Meet Mike

Mike was born and raised in Ottawa, Canada. A great fan of skiing, he was a member of the Quebec ski team and served as a director of a ski school. Mike went on to have a lengthy career in the flooring business. His business trips abroad brought him to Asia, where he traveled to China, Malaysia, Indonesia, and Thailand to source products. Upon retirement, Mike decided to became an entrepreneur, working as the middleman for wood-flooring companies and their clients. As an independent consultant, Mike can now work from anywhere in the world.

Mike now lives in Bangkok, Thailand. He has traded in his skis for a motorcycle and enjoys motorcycle touring in Asia. He has married and enjoys life in Thailand. A cancer survivor, Mike says "I could expand my sourcing business, but it cuts into my riding and exploring the country. My priorities changed after being diagnosed with cancer. Life is short, and I don't want to spend this final stage working too hard."

Overall, my life here is very satisfying. My wife and I enjoy the nightlife of Bangkok, which means international cuisine, movies from everywhere, and live shows and music. (Motorcycle) riding is a big part of my life, and wherever I ride, people are friendly, inquisitive, and extremely helpful.

Riding with my friends from all over the world has exposed me to the country's rich culture and history. I'm enjoying life to its fullest at an age when some of my old friends in Canada are winding theirs down.

Mike

Exercise #3
What is important to me?

(Sometimes we act for internal reasons. These reasons are often based the values we hold and the ideas that we have about what is important in life. Our values can provide an anchor for the decisions we make and how we view our lives.)

For each of the following topics, answer these questions: What is most important to you? What do you most care about?

My work and education:

____

____

____

____

____

____

My relationships with others:

____

____

____

____

____

My personal growth:

____

____

____

____

My health:

My leisure time:

ADJUSTMENT

Moving abroad is a major life change. Adjustment to a new culture tends to improve over time. Making accommodations and changes are a part of the adjustment process.

Cross-cultural adjustment

When we travel abroad, we are inevitably brought into contact with different cultures. This contact brings with it a need to adjust to new cultures. Fortunately, we are already experienced at cultural adjustment. In our work, education, and social lives we have likely already met many people who are different from ourselves and we have subsequently learned to understand and get along with them. Cross-cultural adjustment when moving abroad is substantially the same. We meet people, learn about one another, establish new shared experiences, and make accommodations for our differences. We are likely already good at cross-cultural adjustment, even if we are not aware of it.

One of the differences of cross-cultural adjustment abroad is the variety of differences we encounter. When we make intercultural contact with people who are different from ourselves but from the same country, we each will have a shared reference library of what things mean and how we should act. We may value different things and express these values differently, but, since we have a shared cultural foundation, we generally find our differences few in number and understandable. When we make cross-cultural contact with another culture abroad, we may no longer have a strong, shared, cultural foundation. Instead of a few, understandable differences, we may be faced with a great many differences that are new to us. We can become bewildered and overwhelmed by a variety of differences found across the activities of daily life, work, and social relationships.

Another difference for cross-cultural adjustment abroad is the depth of differences. Not only can we face a great number of differences, but we can also face fundamental differences. The scale of our differences can be great simply because some cultures are intrinsically different. These intrinsic differences may be related to differing core values within each society. For example, Western countries tends to have a more short-term time orientation. This value may be reflected in the phrase, time is money. Other cultures may have a long-term time orientation. They may prioritize other values, such as relationships, over time. Fundamental differences like this are important since they shape how we act and can make it easy to misinterpret the actions and motivations of others across cultures. Viewed from different cultural lenses, one culture may appear to be unresponsive or lazy while the other may appear to be hurried and impudent. Yet, each is acting within its own value system.

The world today is more interconnected than ever before. This global connectivity brings exposure and awareness of people and cultures worldwide. We each have an inherent understanding of our own culture since we were raised in it. But it is likely that we also have mental models of many other cultures across the world. Depending on what positives and negatives we have seen of other cultures in the news, social media, sports, politics, or entertainment, this can either be a great help or a great hinderance to cross-cultural adjustment.

> *Different countries have different customs, and at some point, you'll probably become frustrated by the differences from your home country. If you make an effort to embrace the differences, rather than expect things to be the way they were at home, you'll feel like a local in no time.*
>
> *Katie*

The importance of cross-cultural adjustment

The world, including the world of business, is global. This has increased interest in establishing cross-cultural competence and understanding its benefits, which include increased creativity, innovation, and productivity. A 2019 survey of over 700 corporate board directors in the United States found that directors believed that a culturally diverse corporate board provides unique perspectives (94%), enhances corporate board performance (87%), improves relationships with investors (84%), and enhances the productivity of the company (76%).

While research supports the positive impacts of cultural diversity in the workplace, the results are sometimes mixed. A study conducted by the Institute for the Study of Labor in Germany found that an ethnically diverse workforce had a negative effect on productivity. They proposed that this effect was due to the communication and integration costs associated with maintaining a diverse workforce. These results make sense from the perspective that, while diversity has benefits, these benefits require an investment in order to gain them. Like any other investment, investing in a diverse workforce may take time to provide the desired results.

The business world has learned that relationship and communications skills combined with a people-focused attitude are essential for cross-cultural groups to be effective. These skills also apply at the interpersonal level. But success at any level, business or personal, does not come free. Building cross-cultural competence requires a sincere interest, an openness to new experiences, and a commitment to examine and change how we think, act, and relate to others.

Cross-cultural adjustment also has positive effects on a personal level. Researchers have found that people who report being adjusted also report that they have closer social networks, stronger emotional support and problem-solving networks, and more psychological comfort and well-being. Research tends to find that many expatriates report moderate, but not high, levels of adjustment. This indicates that, while expatriates do adjust to the host nation culture, adjustment challenges may be a persistent feature of living abroad.

Adjustment curve

Cross-cultural adjustment is a process. It begins with cross-cultural contact and ends with our return to our home culture. There are several proposals of how the adjustment curve is shaped. One of the most common curves is the "U" curve. This curve proposes that we begin cross-cultural adjustment in an open-minded and excited state, experience setbacks as we become more fully immersed in a new culture, and then rebound as we make adjustments. Another common curve is the "W" curve. It follows the path of the "U" curve, but adds an additional period of adjustment to account for our return home and re-entry into our culture of origin. Some people believe that the early honeymoon period of adjustment is overrated and propose a "J" curve, where we face adjustment challenges immediately and have to begin adaptation without delay.

The general path of the "W" curve tracks our adjustment challenges from departure to return to our home culture. There are many variations, but the "W" cultural adjustment curve shows how we progress through four phases as we move from initial exposure to adjustment and acceptance and then return home. In general, these four phases are: honeymoon, shock, adjustment, integration, and re-entry.

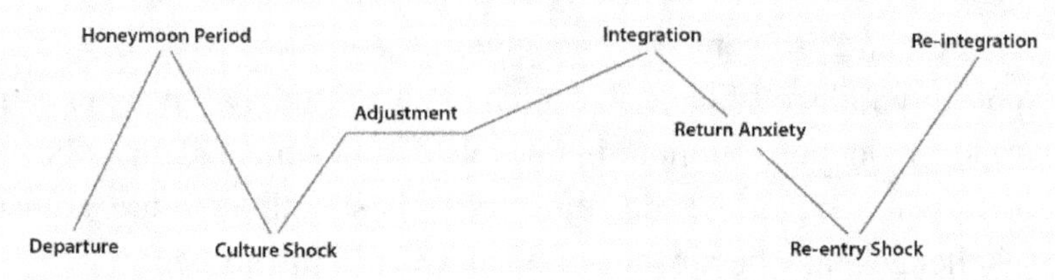

Honeymoon phase

When a person moves abroad, it can be an exciting event. They may be excited and looking forward to the new experience. This positive attitude can carry over once a person is abroad. During the early phase of contact and adjustment, they may still be comfortably resting in their own cultural orientation. Their cultural views may not yet have come into conflict with differences in the host nation culture. Many of the problems of adjusting to daily life may not have surfaced yet and the need to make adjustments and find new solutions may not yet be strong.

> *I don't believe much in the so-called honeymoon period depicted in the famous U-curve of culture shock. For me it's more a J shape. The first months are made of hard work, sometimes loneliness, even frustration and nostalgia for what we have left behind. I always make sure to focus on the reasons that supported our move, the advantages that the move entails, the short- and long-term benefits, career, and academic-wise.*
>
> *Marta*

Shock

As the initial excitement of living abroad begins to wear off, we may experience more and more of the stress associated with adapting to a new lifestyle in a new culture. We may begin to become overwhelmed by the differences we are experiencing and the difficulty of doing even simple daily living tasks in a society that has a different language and different rules for business and social interaction. Culture shock can create feelings of loneliness, depression, confusion, and frustration. It can result in a loss of identity when many of our familiar cultural reference points are lost or changed. Culture shock cannot be completely eliminated, but its negative effects can be softened. Co-mingling cultures does not have to be a battleground. We can turn it into an opportunity to learn, grow, and expand our worldview.

Fortunately, we do not have to remain stuck in our cultural adjustment. Most people find new friends, resolve problems with daily living, and gradually understand more and more about the habits of the local people and the rules of life they go by. Cross-cultural adjustment is a process. We are the agents of our own change. We can make the process faster or slower, or more or less enjoyable. But the path is often not a straight one.

Some expatriates compare cultural adjustment and daily life abroad to a roller-coaster ride. Culture shock is not limited to a certain time or certain stage of adjustment. It can continue to happen anytime while living abroad. At times we may feel like we are beginning to feel at home or that we are getting used to the host country's culture, then we may encounter something new and find ourselves having to pause and adapt once again.

> *The most challenging part of being an expat is dealing with loneliness and isolation. When you move to a new country, loneliness can be unbearable. It can make the start of an expat life a terrible experience. The best things I did after moving country were making friends and learning survival phrases of the local language. It helped me tremendously in dealing with loneliness and isolation. To my surprise, it helped with settling in as well.*
>
> *Jenny*

Spotlight on culture
Time

Perceptions of time, and the value of time, differ across cultures. Monochronic (mono = one, chronic = time) cultures perceive time as a single continuum. They may value punctuality and prefer to complete tasks in order. Monochronic cultures tend to be low context. Examples of monochronic cultures include the United States, Canada, Britain, much of western Europe. But there is a lot of variations across all cultures worldwide.

Polychronic (poly = many, chronic = time) cultures view time in many different ways and do not view punctuality as important. They may be comfortable working on several tasks at the same time and leaving one task incomplete while beginning another. Polychronic cultures tend to be high context. Examples of polychronic cultures include Arab cultures, Latin America, Brazil, the Philippines, and many African countries.

Views on time can be shaped by other values. In some cultures, social obligations and relationships may simply be more important than work-related responsibilities. So, time may be prioritized differently when competing social and work responsibilities need to be resolved.

Meet: Tal

Originally from Israel, Tal moved with her Canadian husband to his hometown in Canada, leaving her television career behind. She is now a self-styled entrepreneur and stay-at-home mom. Tal was 35 years old at time of the move and a mother of one child aged 2 and pregnant with her second child. The move was made to allow her husband to return home and join a family busines operating in Toronto. Tal admits that moving in the middle of the Canadian winter was not the best move. But she discovered that she loved the Canadian winter and found it refreshing after growing up in Israel where temperatures can reach 45 Celsius (113 Fahrenheit).

Starting a new life in a new country, Tal found that being a stay-at-home mom was not enough for her. She continued to follow her lifelong dream of finding emotional and financial freedom. After a up and down journey of three years she is currently the owner of an online business where she helps people, especially expatriate women, learn the skills and foundations of managing a digital business. Her online business also allows her to follow another dream, building a family. As Tal says, "It's not just about the money, it's about the lifestyle."

I have to say that to leaving my 12-year career behind, in Israel, was the most difficult thing for me. I was working as a producer at a TV children's channel and I studied for a long time to get the position I was in. It was literally as if I had lost my career and all the meaning that I had as a TV producer and a career woman disappeared.

Tal

Exercise #4
Culture shock inventory

(Culture shock can impact our moods, how we feel, and how we react to our environment.)

Since you have moved abroad, have you had:

YES/NO   Changes in eating habits (eating more or less)?
YES/NO   Changes in sleeping habits?
YES/NO   Feelings of loneliness or isolation?
YES/NO   Acute homesickness?
YES/NO   Calling home much more often than usual?
YES/NO   Feeling hostile towards others?
YES/NO   Avoiding or minimizing contact with locals?
YES/NO   Staying home more frequently or for longer periods?
YES/NO   Complaining frequently about the host country?
YES/NO   Feelings of irritability, sadness, or depression?
YES/NO   Frequent feelings of frustration?
YES/NO   Periods of being easily angered?
YES/NO   More frequent or increased use of alcohol?
YES/NO   Use of alcohol or drugs to feel better?
YES/NO   Self-doubts?
YES/NO   A sense of failure?
YES/NO   Recurring illness?
YES/NO   A lowered sense of energy or motivation?
YES/NO   Withdrawing from friends or activities?

The unpleasant feelings associated with culture shock are temporary, natural, and similar to the stress we may experience with any other transition that we may go through in our lives. We can be patient and give ourselves time to work through the adjustment process. What activities or actions can you take to feel better and increase your self-confidence and self-motivation?

____

____

____

____

____

____

____

____

> *Today I've been living outside my home country for over 20 years. I've done eight international moves and lived on four continents. I've woken up in the small hours of the morning not knowing what city or even country I am in. There have been moments paralyzed with fear, overwhelmed with information, and dizzy with excitement. Culture shock is my drug and I cannot get enough.*
>
> *Antoine*

Adjustment

We may begin adjustment by relaxing and realizing that our initial feelings of frustration, anxiety, and confusion are a natural and normal part of reacting to the challenges of living abroad. As we live abroad longer, the feeling of being overwhelmed by the changes around us begins to subside and our ability to understand the host nation culture and navigate the tasks of daily life increase. Everyday activities such as shopping, taking a taxi, and going to work or school are no longer major problems. Although we may not yet be fluent in the local language, we can communicate introductions and express basic needs. We may still be dependent on allies such as locals and other expatriates to help us, but we are increasingly comfortable and self-confident being on our own.

The period of initial adjustment is a crossroads. We can continue adapting to the new situation by remaining open to learning and trying new things. This often requires that we pay attention to those around us, become better at cross-cultural communication, and stay flexible and open-minded as we respond to new situations. It may also mean that we are willing to take risks and make mistakes as we ask questions and try new behaviors to understand and match the local culture.

However, some people can reach a cultural plateau in early adjustment that they do not substantially move from during their time abroad. They may achieve sufficient survival skills for daily living but do not expand their skills much further. They may not achieve full autonomy and may remain dependent on key locals, other expatriates, or other support mechanisms for assistance. They may retain a sense of separation and isolation, frustration, or a general lack of enjoyment with living abroad. Remaining at a cultural plateau is largely a personal decision that can be changed by re-energizing our interest in the local culture and our life abroad, improving our language skills, meeting new people, and trying new things.

Integration

Once people have lived abroad for a longer period of time, they may achieve a level of integration with the host nation culture. They are comfortable interacting with locals and giving advice to other expatriates about how to live here.

The key features of the integration phase of cultural adjustment are acceptance and mastery. We have a more complete understanding of the host nation culture and we have learned how to live within it. At this stage we have established a routine for work, school, daily, and social life. We know how to navigate the local environment to get what we need and to solve problems. We have a deeper understanding of the habits, customs, food, people, and characteristics of the host nation and accept them. We feel comfortable with both our local and expatriate friends and with the local language.

Integration means to become a part of. During this phase of adjustment, we have developed an understanding of not only what locals do but why they do it. This understanding allows us to participate more meaningfully with locals and the host nation culture. We begin to merge our culture and the local culture together as we adopt local practices and attitudes and integrate them with our own identities and behaviors. At this stage we are comfortable with living abroad, we may become reluctant to think about going home and may make a decision of live abroad longer or permanently.

Returning home

The term repatriation is used to describe the process of returning home from living abroad. When we return home, we may begin the process of cultural adjustment all over again in the form of re-entry shock or reverse culture shock. Since we have made adjustments to living abroad, it makes sense that we would naturally need to make re-adjustments once we return to our culture of origin. Surprisingly, some returning expatriates report that reverse culture shock can be more difficult than the initial culture shock of traveling abroad. Reverse culture shock can be affected by the length of time we have spent away, how much of local culture we have adopted, the degree to which we have maintained cultural contact with home, where we are in life, and any changes to life roles that may have occurred. For example, if we left our culture of origin as a single student and returned as a married, working adult, we may be more accustomed to the work culture abroad than to that at home.

Exercise #5
Where am I on the adjustment curve?

One way of looking at adjustment is to think about where we are on the adjustment curve. Select response that best describes you.

A. I have not been in the country for very long. I am still excited to be here and learning a lot of new things.

B. I have been in the country for a while. I have found that living here is harder than I expected. I thought things would be different here.

C. I have been in country for a while. I am finally learning how to live here. I don't know everything but I understand the ups and downs better than before.

D. I have lived in the country for a long time. I am comfortable interacting with locals and giving others advice about how to live here.

The responses match the following positions on the culture curve:
A. Honeymoon; B. Culture shock; C. Adjustment; D. Integration.

What position on the culture curve matches your response? Do you think it accurately describes you? Why or why not? If you looked at the choices and felt that none or several of them applied to you, how would you describe how you feel about being in the country? How would you assess your skills at daily living?

____

____

____

____

Spotlight on culture
Personal space

United States
One of the cross-cultural differences between societies is how we view personal space. In North America, people generally view the first 18 inches of space around them as intimate space. This space is where people conduct intimate activities. The space between 18 inches and 4 feet is generally considered personal distance. In this arm's length space, people interact with close friends and coworkers. The space between 4 and 12 feet is social distance, a common zone in more formal social and business gatherings. Beyond 12 feet is public distance, where more formal interactions such large meetings occur. Americans are accustomed to physical space and may become territorial if they feel crowded, snapping at people who push in line and staking out room for themselves, whether it's their desk, train seat, or airplane seat.

China
Chinese have close personal space to each other when compared to people from the United States. Chinese in urban areas are used to a lack of personal space. Cities are densely populated and crowded, especially on public transportation. Shared housing is common until children marry.

The total lack of personal space in China gets under an American's skin in a matter of seconds. Riding a bus designed for 40 people, with close to 100 crammed in it is a daily test of my cultural sensitivity.

Tom

Predictors of adjustment

Adjusting to living abroad is a complex process. While some researchers chose to focus on single factor of adjustment, the vast majority of research examines multiple factors of adjustment. This is consistent with the view that cross-cultural adjustment is multi-dimensional. There are many changes to adapt to, so it is understandable that there would have a lot of internal and external factors involved in the adjustment process.

While an immense number of adjustment factors have been examined, we will focus on a selected number. Some of these factors will contribute to adjustment in expected ways, others have more surprising effects. We will look at the following factors: language, self-efficacy, relationship skills, spouse adjustment, cultural distance, role clarity, and previous experience.

Language

Some research has found that foreign language skills have a positive effect on cultural adjustment, but the research findings are not consistent. In some cases, foreign language skills have not been found to be significantly related to work adjustment. The importance of foreign language skills may be situationally dependent, as some work environments abroad, especially those employing expatriates, more commonly use English and some do not. Interestingly, research has found that an interest in learning the local language, regardless of language skill, has been found to be positively related to cultural adjustment. It may be that a willingness to learn a language may be just one manifestation of an overall openness to the new environment. It is not surprising that research has also found that foreign language skills are positively related to frequency of contact with local nationals and satisfaction with contact with local nationals. As language skills increase, contact with local nationals increases and people tend to be happier with their contacts.

Self-efficacy

Self-efficacy is the belief we have in our own abilities. Most people understand this term as self-confidence. Self-efficacy is different than self-esteem. Self-esteem concerns our overall feelings of our worth and value. Self-efficacy concerns our view of our ability to meet challenges and complete tasks successfully. Higher levels of self-efficacy are positively related to all dimensions of adjustment abroad.

Relationship skills

Research shows that relationship skills have a strong, positive effect on all dimensions of adjustment. Relationship skills connect us to other people in a meaningful way. Research has found that when expatriates receive interpersonal support, they have better adjustment, less stress and anxiety, improved psychological well-being, as well as less emotional exhaustion and feelings of burn-out.

Spouse adjustment

For expatriates who are married, research shows that spouse adjustment is the single most critical variable in predicting all dimensions of expatriate adjustment. If a spouse is not adjusting well to living abroad, it tends to have cascading effects on your own adjustment. This is not surprising since spouses share living arrangements, share problems and concerns with each other, and depend on each other for support.

Cultural distance

The degree to which an expatriate's country of origin and the host nation are culturally different has been measured in research as cultural distance or as cultural novelty. It is hypothesized that when the two cultures are significantly different, adjustment is more difficult. Research has verified this hypothesis. Researchers have found that an increase in differences between cultures leads to increased symptoms of anxiety and more difficulty in adjusting.

Role clarity

For expatriates who are working abroad, role clarity has been found to be substantially and positively related to work adjustment. When expatriates move abroad, they encounter a new environment with many uncertainties. It makes sense that clearly defined work roles help reduce the overall uncertainty and helps expatriates adjust at work. Expatriates who experience higher levels of co-worker support have higher levels of work adjustment. However, when expatriates experience role conflict due to uncertain work role or job expectations, adjusting to work abroad is more difficult and adjustment levels are lower.

Previous experience

Expatriates with more previous experience generally have higher levels of adjustment. Although previous experience living abroad has a positive effect on adjustment, its effect may be small. One interesting meta-analytic review of many different studies found that previous experience contributed just a few percentage points to adjustment. One possible explanation for this small effect may be that each country, culture, and expatriate experience contain enough unique factors, challenges, and conditions that it limits the amount of experience that can be directly transferred.

I'm very proud of my Dutch and Polish heritage. It's one of the first things I discuss with people when we first meet. It's a big part of my identity, even after living in the USA for almost fifteen years. I continue to speak both languages with my parents, extended family and friends.

Nicolette

Exercise #6
How do I describe myself?

Do you fit into one of these categories? Do you fit into several categories? If not, how do you describe myself?

___ Foreign worker (working abroad for a company back home)
___ Foreign recruit (recruited by a local company)
___ Entrepreneur (I started my own business here)
___ Greener pastures (living abroad for a better life)
___ Retiree (I chose to retire here)
___ Dreamer (It was always my dream to live here)
___ Student (I am here for training or education)
___ Lifelong learner (I am here to learn on my own)
___ Romantic (looking for love or a relationship)
___ Family expat (I want my children to live abroad)
___ Traveling partner (I followed my spouse or partner)
___ Adventurer (I am seeking excitement and new experiences)
___ Career expat (I always work abroad, for a company or myself)
___ Cultural chameleon (I totally adopted a new culture)
___ Refugee (life circumstances forced me the leave home)
___ Missionary (I am here to make a positive contribution)
___ Back to my roots (I am here to explore my family culture)
___ ____________________________________(Other)

How do you describe yourself? What is your primary reason for living abroad? When others look at you, how do they describe you?

____

____

____

____

Exercise #7
My groups

(How do you see yourself? How do you think others see you?)

Think about and write down ALL the different groups to which you belong. Another way to think of this might be to consider all the different labels that could be applied to you, or all the different roles you fulfill in your life.

____

____

____

____

____

Now, write down all the stereotypes for these groups. One way to approach this is to apply this statement to each group, "Everybody knows that (group) ____________."

____

____

____

____

____

How do you think what you say and do influences the attitudes of others towards you?

____

____

____

____

____

COPING

Coping is how we deal with the problems we face. It begins with a stress or a demand that we must react to and follows an adaptive process as we apply different mental, emotional, and behavioral strategies to manage stress and achieve a desirable outcome.

Stress

Although we tend to view stress as an event or condition that causes us to energize our resources to combat it, stress ranges from the normal reactions of our bodies to the wear and tear of everyday living to the mental and emotional burdens we carry that arise from the problems we face. Stress is any life event or change that demands a response, adjustment, or adaptation. In a sense, stress itself in neutral. Stress is any demand, good or bad, that is placed on us. It can be positive or negative, short-term or long-term. It is simply the things that happen to us or the conditions we face. It is how we interpret events and how we react to them that creates what we feel as stress. Different people interpret things differently, some viewing things as more stressful, some viewing things as less stressful.

We all know that negative events can cause stress. Negative stress can either be short-term or long-term. If we do not turn off our stress mechanism or mitigate the stress, it can take a toll on our physical, mental, and emotional health. Positive stress can activate our survival mechanisms as well as provide extra momentum for action and boost productivity. Examples include being hungry, being excited, anxious, or focused on performing well in work, school, or sports, feeling energized to reach a goal, even the motivation we feel when searching for a new home or planning for a holiday or a vacation.

The physical, mental, and emotional conditions we face are constantly changing. Sometimes we are under stress from things that happen directly to us, but we can also have feelings of stress from things that happen in the environment around us and to others that we know.

We live with stress every moment of our lives and have adapted to it either consciously or unconsciously. We can be more susceptible to stress under certain conditions:

- If we have poor lifestyle habits such as not eating, sleeping, or exercising appropriately, or drinking alcohol above safe limits.
- When we are already under stress and we experience new, additional stresses.
- When we have been previously exposed to traumatic experiences.
- When a stressful event occurs unexpectedly and we are caught off-guard and surprised by it.
- When we lack close friends that we can talk to or we are socially isolated.
- If we have a tendency to avoid feelings, withdraw, or assign blame to others during stressful situations.
- If we have difficulty expressing our feelings.
- When we are not prepared or lack the resources to handle problems that we face.
- When exposure to stress is constant or intense.

We cannot avoid stress in our lives, but we can minimize its negative impact by how we cope with it. This is an essential, perhaps life-saving, skill. If we do not learn how to respond to stress, it will persist and can eventually lead to exhaustion, physically, mentally, or emotionally. It is a natural human reaction to distance ourselves from stress, so we may develop an indifferent or cynical attitude as a protective barrier. We may have a fight or flight response, depending on whether we want to avoid or to tackle the stress. Sometimes, we are simply frozen by stress, and our ability to react, make decisions, or move forward is paralyzed.

> *The loneliness of the expatriate is an odd and complicated thing, for it is inseparable from the feeling of being free, of having escaped.*
>
> *Adam*

What is coping?

What is your first reaction when suddenly faced with stress? Do you talk about it with your friends? Make a plan to overcome it? Avoid confronting the situation by putting it aside to deal with later? Find relief by having comfort food or a drink? All of these are ways in which we cope with a stress, difficulty, burden, or problem by either adopting a strategy to deal with the stress itself, or by trying to manage its emotional impact upon us. Although some of these strategies are more beneficial than the others, they all have some value. Each one has a potential role to serve in the total landscape of all of our options. The key is applying an appropriate strategy, at the appropriate time, for the appropriate length of time.

There are many factors that shape coping. When we have trouble coping with a problem, we may have feelings of anxiousness, apprehension, dread, fearfulness, or depression. We might lack information or have an incorrect perception of what is happening and why. We might have difficulty or lack the desire to ask for help or seek support. In general, when we have trouble coping, there is a mismatch between the problem, our available coping resources, and our response. The problem simply overwhelms our ability to handle it in some way.

We tend to cope with problems more effectively when we have available resources to help us solve problems and manage our emotions. These can be friends and allies that have faced similar problems and are available to talk and listen to us. We also tend to cope better when we have confidence in our own abilities and have a sense of control over what is happening. Having clear goals helps us think more clearly, organize our thoughts, focus on solutions, and manage our expectations. It helps if our basic needs for food, sleep, exercise, and companionship met and are we not involved in destructive, risky, or unhealthy behaviors.

Coping may be different for expatriates. This is because expatriates may be in new and radically different cultural environments where they face a whole range of issues, large and small, that require a coping response. Expatriates may face long-term issues, such as finding safe housing and employment, face multiple issues simultaneously, such as learning to shop, get around in a new area, and navigate local bureaucracies, and may face additional problems before other issues are resolved. This can add to the total weight of the stress we face and it can strain our ability to cope and manage survival tasks and daily life.

> *The joy of life comes from our encounters with new experiences, and hence there is no greater joy than to have an endlessly changing horizon, for each day to have a new and different sun.*
>
> *Christopher*

Coping is a process

Our reaction to stress is essentially a survival mechanism. It enables is to take action quickly when under threat of harm. Unfortunately, we also feel stress when we are not directly under physical threat, such as when we are running late or an appointment, are having difficulty being understood by others, have a heavy workload, or cannot achieve a desired goal. We have to have some way to manage and cope with stress.

General adaptation syndrome
The term general adaptation syndrome is the formal term for how our bodies react to stress. The term was coined by Hans Selye, a Hungarian doctor and researcher, to capture the physical reaction of our bodies to stress. It is also sometimes applied more generally to our reactions to stress. The general adaptation syndrome is a process that consists of 3 phases: alarm, resistance, and exhaustion.

In the alarm phase, we experience an event or demand that we perceive as stressful. Our bodies activate a physical response to energize resources that we will need for a fight or flight response. These responses include reactions such as a higher heart rate, increased respiration, and higher blood sugar levels. Should the stress persist, we enter a resistance phase where our bodies maintain a higher metabolic rate to help keep us prepared to counter the stress. Our bodies cannot maintain this higher metabolic rate indefinitely, so when we are under a persistent stress or threat our bodies may tire, become susceptible to sickness, or its ability to respond may weaken or collapse.

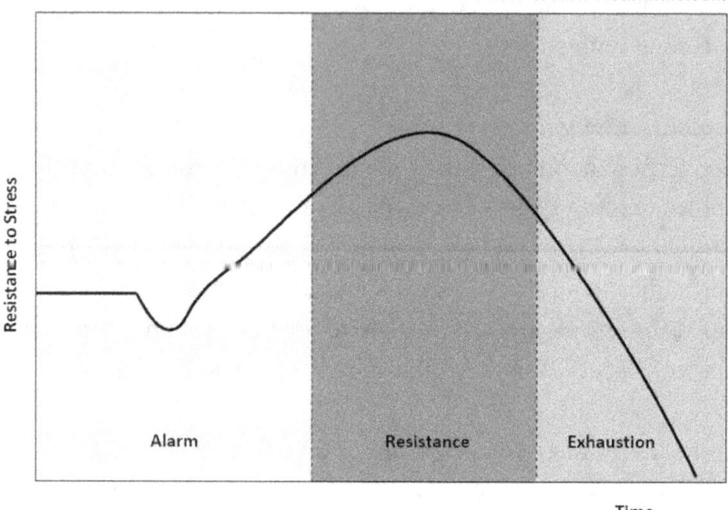

Coping

Coping is a process of anticipation, demand, appraisal, and reaction. Coping includes our physical reactions to stress, but also includes how we perceive and react to stress; how we think, appraise, and perceive events and conditions that are occurring around us. It would be simple if our responses occurred in an orderly sequence. But in reality, we live in a dynamic world. Different things are constantly happening simultaneously to us and around us. Our focus and our mental state are constantly shifting, changing the way we think and the way we cope.

There are many different approaches to understanding how we cope. Some are based on our internal characteristics, such as personality, self-confidence, or emotional control. Some are based on external factors, such as social support or prior experience living abroad. And, some are based on how we react. For example, we may try to avoid or repress the stress or we may try to actively address and resolve the stress.

Richard Lazarus and Susan Folkman, both from the United States, created a comprehensive approach to understanding coping that viewed coping as a transaction between a person, including multiple systems such as cognitive, physiological, emotional, psychological, neurological, and the complex environment they live in. They characterized eight active coping strategies:

- Self-Control. We try to control our emotions in response to stress.
- Confrontation. We face the stress and take action to change the situation and bring it back to our favor.
- Social support. We talk to others and look for social connections to help us survive a difficult time.
- Emotional distancing. We stay indifferent to what is going on around and prevent the stress from controlling our actions.
- Escape and avoidance. We minimize or deny the existence of stress.
- Radical acceptance. We use unconditional self-acceptance to adapt to adversity.
- Positive reappraisal. We seek to find the answer in the difficulty and grow from it.
- Strategic problem-solving. We implement specific solution-focused strategies to get through the difficulty and redirect our actions.

Appraisal

An important element of coping is how we appraise the stress. It is not uncommon for two people faced with the same stress to have different responses. This is due to their differing interpretations of the stress. Some people may interpret an event or condition as more threatening and have a stronger response to it, others less so. Lazarus and Folkman developed the concept of cognitive appraisal and reappraisal. According to this theory, coping with stress includes our internal processes of thinking and assigning meaning to stressful events. This concept is important. If we can increase our understanding of what is happening to us and around us, and change how we think, then we can change the meaning of stress and shape how we cope with it.

> *The best thing we did for ourselves was made friends with Thai locals: our favorite smoothie lady; the guy that gasses up our motorbike; the guesthouse owner we now hang out with at least once a week. Whatever Thai we learned was reinforced through our new friends. It's a great way to gain confidence living in Thailand and learn about what goes on in life below the surface.*
>
> *Angela*

Meet Max

Max is a German working in Poland. His 26 years old and a graduate of the Deggendorf Institute of Technology with a degree in Applied Economics. He works at IBM in Poland as an account analyst. When Max graduated college, he was only offered internships, not the full-time employment he was seeking. Max took the opportunity to gain work experience outside of Germany, in part because of his friendships with foreign exchange students he had met in Germany.

With the help of his Polish partner he shifted his focus to Poland. Max discovered that his German language skills were in high demand there. His position at IBM was specifically designed for the German market and was language dependent. Max received positive responses so quickly that he had to borrow a suit for his interview. Max says he has never regretted starting his career in Poland. He believes it has given him the chance to meet a new culture and gain work experience he might not have been able to access in his own country.

There are two things I would recommend to everybody, first of all, it would be open to new things. For example, even though we are neighboring countries, there is always something new to discover. I mean the differences in culture or how to approach problems. The second is to learn the language of the country as well as possible. Even if it is only a few phrases, it will prove useful. This is especially important when it comes to bureaucracy because with a little knowledge of Polish everything goes much faster.

Max

Exercise #8
My strengths

Think of a time when you proactively took some action to reduce
stress or solve a problem and it turned out well.

____

____

____

____

Try to recall the personal strengths and abilities that helped you
successfully cope with the situation.

____

____

____

____

____

List how you feel your strengths have shaped your personality and
how you cope with stress and challenges.

____

____

____

____

____

Identify the core strengths that you generally tend to use during
stressful situations. Now try to think of other situations where you
can use these strengths to adapt in a positive manner.

____

____

____

Exercise #9
How I cope

(This exercise uses a few items from an assessment questionnaire called the COPE Inventory. The COPE Inventory is used to assess two different coping strategies people use to respond to stress.)

Here is a list of ways to cope with a situation. Select YES if you usually use the approach. Select NO if you do not usually use the approach. Choose the answer that reflects what you actually do.

YES/NO 1. I try to get advice from someone about what to do.
YES/NO 2. I talk to someone to find out more about the situation.
YES/NO 3. I talk to someone who could do something concrete
         about the problem.
YES/NO 4. I ask people who have had similar experiences what
         they did.
YES/NO 5. I discuss my feelings with someone.
YES/NO 6. I try to get emotional support from friends or relatives.
YES/NO 7. I get sympathy and understanding from someone.
YES/NO 8. I talk to someone about how I feel.

In this exercise, items 1 through 4 relate to how we use social support to help solve problems. Items 5 through 8 relate to how we use social support to help manage our emotions. What approaches do you most often use? Why do you think you prefer them?

____

____

____

____

____

____

COPING STRATEGIES

There are many different strategies for coping with the stresses of living abroad in a new cultural environment. There are essentially two fundamental approaches for the different strategies. We can either change our environment to suit ourselves or we can change ourselves to suit the environment. The first approach includes direct actions such as problem solving or modifying our immediate environment. The second approach includes changing our feelings, perceptions, and appraisals of our environment. In this section, we will examine eight specific strategies that include elements of both approaches.

While we will focus on positive, healthy strategies, we must recognize that sometimes, when we are under stress, we can adopt unhealthy coping strategies. Many times, unhealthy coping strategies are overly avoidant or defensive. The problem with these strategies is that they do not face and resolve the problem. A problem that is left unresolved often becomes increasingly difficult to resolve, which can encourage us to delay resolution even longer. Unhealthy coping responses often provide immediate relief, but can have negative long-term consequences. Unhealthy coping responses include excessive drug and alcohol use, overeating, procrastinating, sleeping too much or too little, social withdrawal, rationalization, denial, and aggression.

However, sometimes problems threaten to overwhelm us. In this case, it can be therapeutic to temporarily set a problem aside so we can gain emotional control and prepare for it. A small break can give us time to think and help us regain our sense of balance and control. But the key is that our avoidance is only temporary, that we use our time to strengthen our emotional, social, and other resources, and that we return to address the problem as soon we are better prepared, even though it may not be comfortable to face.

We will look at the following coping strategies:

- Prepare
- Watch and learn
- Get connected
- Change how you think
- Solve problems
- Feel better
- Keep the big picture in mind
- Define your story.

> *National culture cannot be changed, but you should understand and respect it.*
>
> *Professor Geert Hofstede*

STRATEGY #1: Prepare

When you are preparing to move abroad, it is helpful to first think about why you are moving. What is the purpose? What do you want to do, acquire, or achieve? What is your goal? The value of a purpose or goal is that it gives us something we can begin to plan for. So, it can help translate an abstract idea into something more concrete and achievable. You know where you are at. With a goal, you will know where we want to go. It is helpful to write your goals down. When we write down our goals, we are more likely to achieve them. Writing down a goal forces us to think clearly and specifically about what we want to achieve and helps motivate us to achieve it. Having goals can also provide us an anchor should we get distracted from what we are doing. It helps us re-orient ourselves, sort out what we are doing, and stay focused on what is important to us.

One of the best things we can do to prepare for any life change is to sit down and conduct an honest self-assessment. What do we want to achieve in a practical sense? What are we looking for emotionally? Are we moving to escape a negative or are we moving to get closer to something positive in our lives? What are our strengths and weaknesses? Where have we succeeded or failed in the past and why? When will we know we are happy? Questions like these help us sort out what our sources of motivation and inspiration, realistically assess what we can and cannot reasonably achieve, and understand what a happy life truly means to us. They also help us look at areas for self-improvement before moving abroad.

Part of preparing to live abroad involves thinking about your new life and beginning to open your mind to new things. We can anticipate new changes that we will face and begin to make mental adjustments for them even before we relocate. This anticipatory adjustment is closely related to visualization. When we anticipate a change or visualize a success, it helps increase our self-confidence that we can achieve it.

When you are preparing for a new life, it is helpful to look at a lot of pictures, videos. The visual shock of suddenly being in a new environment can be strong, in some cases almost startling. It is especially important to look at as many images, pictures, and videos as you can. Visual depictions like these leave a strong impression on our brains and can help mitigate the visual shock we will encounter when we step into a completely new environment.

> *When I first went overseas – and I've been an expat for going on for 20 years now – the internet was in its infancy. Today's social networking technologies (Facebook, Twitter, What's App, etc.) offer incredible opportunities to build connections with your new location before you even step on the plane. This wasn't possible when I first went overseas in the early 1990s.*
>
> *Nigel*

In the last decade, there has been an explosion of blogs and vlogs on the internet about foreign travel, living abroad, and expatriate life. Read the biographies of successful expatriates and the stories that others have shared on the internet. These internet sources are often first-hand accounts of living abroad. They are often provided in the context of the expatriate experience. For example, a following spouse living abroad with a working partner may discuss issues with children or families. An adventurous expatriate may catalog his travels and experiences with finding entertainment, romance, housing, or dealing with different money exchange rates. The key is that these are often the stories of people's lives. We have a natural instinct to understand new information when we receive it in the form of a story or in narratives like these.

The life experiences of others are important tools since they can both inform and inspire. When you are preparing for a new life, research and talk to others. Researching and talking to others arms us with knowledge, but it also helps orient us to practical survival tricks and tips. Gaining knowledge can help us manage our expectations and start changes early, especially changes in language, diet, and observation. It also is helpful to start thinking about barriers you may encounter and how you can overcome them. There are a wide variety of expatriate groups available on the internet. Many times, they share country-specific stories, lessons learned, and have open forums to ask questions about how problems can be handled. There is a dual benefit. The forums are a source of information, but they are also a way to connect to the expatriate community and build relationships.

> *Before moving, I remember having funny conversations with fellow foreigners who expected I would see lots of cowboys and eat mostly hamburgers while in the USA.*
>
> *Nicolette*

> *Do as much research as you can before you move so you might be able to know what to expect. I was researching Tilburg and the Netherlands as soon as we found out it was a possibility (maybe a year before we actually moved). I made contact with other people who lived there via Twitter, followed expat blogs and signed up with a local expat club before we even left the States.*
>
> *Andrew*

Exercise #10
What are my goals?

(When we want to improve our lives, setting goals helps us focus and stay on track. But they work best when they are specific.)

Respond to the following questions:

What do you want to achieve or do in the future to be happier?

____
____
____
____
____

Why is achieving it personally important to you?

____
____
____
____
____

When do you want to achieve it?

____
____
____
____
____

How will you know when you have achieved it? What will be different?

____
____

What can you do right now to start working towards it?

Exercise #11
Self-assessment

(We can begin preparation by conducting a thorough self-assessment. Sometimes when we inventory our lives, we find that we have hidden strengths.)

Respond to the following questions.

What problems have I faced in the past?

____

____

____

____

____

What successful coping strategies have I used in the past?

____

____

____

____

____

What unsuccessful coping strategies have I used in the past?

____

____

____

____

____

What are my strengths and abilities that will help me to cope in the future?

____

____

____

____

____

What weaknesses do I have that either make coping or problem-solving difficult or need some improvement?

____

____

____

____

____

What new abilities can I begin to acquire now to help me cope with living abroad?

____

____

____

____

____

STRATEGY #2: Watch and learn

Whether we realize it or not we are in learning mode every moment of our lives. We are constantly receiving signals from the world around us and storing them in our minds. We either store these inputs in categories that we already understand or we mark them as unusual and begin to sort them out, either consciously or unconsciously. Our minds have a tendency to fit what we sense into patterns that we already understand.

Part of the problem is that these patterns may be different or have different meanings in different parts of the world. In many parts of the world, a barking dog is part of the natural rhythm of the day and can be especially common throughout the night. It may not attract special attention. In the United States, a barking dog tends to be unusual, so it stands out and can attract more inquisitive attention. An American may wonder what is happening and investigate. A foreigner may sleep soundly through the sound of a barking dog, while an American is awakened and perhaps made irritable.

We can learn about a new culture or environment in different ways that bring new information and experiences to us. Before departure or after arrival we may attend some cultural or language training online, at work, or through a university course. We may self-educate by actively reading, studying, or researching on our own. We may learn by observing others. This can be through entertainment, social media, or looking at online content. We may directly observe locals, other expatriates, family members, friends, classmates, and coworkers. Finally, we may simply learn through trial and error as we test out new behaviors and reflect on the results.

Observational learning is deceptively simple. We simply look, observe, and learn. When we look at something, we focus on it and give it our attention. This attention helps us to take in the details that we see. Observing includes taking in not only what is happening, but also the content in which it is happening, the dynamics that are occurring between people, and the result. Learning brings the observation home to us. It gives us an awareness and understanding of what we have seen and the actions that have taken place. This understanding provides us a benchmark and a guide for our own future actions.

> *What makes expat life so addictive is that every boring and mundane activity you experience at home, like grocery shopping, commuting to work, or picking up the dry cleaning is, when to move to a foreign country, suddenly transformed into an exciting adventure.*
>
> *Reannon*

There are many ways to observe and learn from the environment around us while living abroad.

Active listening

When we are talking with others it is helpful if we focus our attention on the conversation. This skill is sometimes called active listening. Part of the problem with listening is that we often have a lot of distractions. These distractions can include what is happening in our own mind as we struggle to both understand what is being said and to formulate a response. The resulting logjam can make it more difficult for us to learn and to communicate well. Active listening involves setting aside our instinct to form a response and just focus on what is being said. This includes being attentive to the context, emotion, and non-verbal cues that come along with information. Active listening is the difference between hearing someone and listening to someone. It helps us connect to others and to understand what is going on around us.

Practice observation

We pass by and through many situations as we go through our day. We can make a dedicated effort to practice observing what is going on around us. Perhaps we are in crowded restaurant or market. How do people wait? Are they patient or impatient? Do they form a line? How do they attract a waitress or vendor? What verbal expressions or physical gestures do they use? Locals are using patterns of behavior they have been exposed to since birth. We can focus our attention on these patterns, both big and small, and learn. Noticing and absorbing the little details of daily life can broaden our awareness and understanding of our environment.

Observe social interactions

It is especially helpful for us to observe how people interact when together. All cultures have unwritten social rules. These social rules can change depending on the age, gender, and social status of the individuals. Social rules cover every imaginable interaction, from greetings and introductions, asking and responding to a question, to saying goodbye. It is important to observe, learn, and respect social rules since violations of accepted rules can be interpreted as rude, inconsiderate, or disrespectful, even if that is not our intention. This can damage our attempt to interact with others and may create a hostile reaction.

Take field trips

Part of the fun and adventure of living abroad is having new experiences. Sometimes these experiences just happen to us as we live our lives. Sometimes we seek them out. But our experiences do not have to be major adventures. We can take simple excursions to experience daily living first hand. A field trip can be a visit to any place where you can observe what is happening and try new things out for yourself. It can be as simple as bravely taking a bus by yourself for the first time, going to a new market with a friend, going to a sporting event, or going out for a coffee with the intent to talk to and interact with locals in order to practice your language skills. Field trips are not only fun, but they can also build our self-confidence.

Look for meaning

Observing what is happening around us is just the first step in understanding it. We have to go one step further. In addition to knowing what is happening, we have to try to understand why it is happening. This means we have to look for the meaning behind what we see. Sometimes we may need to set our own values and perceptions aside and open our minds. We all have our own pattern for assessing and judging what is happening around us. We can be aware and mindful of our own judgmental instincts and, rather than judging or criticizing, we can try to understand why others think and act as they do.

Make your own adjustments

Sometimes when we move abroad, we find ourselves in an environment that is much more fast or slow paced than we are used to. We can observe how locals have adapted and make a decision whether their strategies are suited for us. But it may be necessary to set some limits to protect and preserve your personal time and space. You may need to prioritize important tasks and stop or decrease involvement in other, less important activities. You may need to schedule some time for yourself in your daily or weekly routine so you can re-energize and maintain a personal balance. You may need to set boundaries for involvement in work or social activities and use firm communication to prevent your boundaries from being violated.

Sometimes we may need to practice patience when things are going at a different speed than we are used to.

Regardless, make sure to keep an open mind. Living abroad is genuinely a wonderful experience, a lifestyle that exposes you to new cultures and different perspectives. Embrace it and dive right in. Additionally, when in doubt, do as the locals do. See how they're living and how they act. How do they commute? What do they eat? What do they wear? And don't be afraid to ask questions.

Jessica

Exercise #12
My learning styles

There are three basic learning preferences: visual (V), auditory or hearing (A), kinetic such as touching and doing (K). For each question below, mark what you usually do.

When I assemble an object, I usually.
__ (V) Look at the picture first, and then read the instructions
__ (A) I read the instructions or talk out loud as I work
__ (K) I usually ignore the directions and figure it out as I go along

When I try to concentrate, I usually:
__ (V) Get distracted by clutter or movement
__ (A) Get distracted by sounds and control the sounds around me
__ (K) Become distracted by activity and commotion around me

When I relax, I prefer most to:
__ (V) Watch a movie, go to see something
__ (A) Listen to music, read, talk to a friend
__ (K) Play sports, make crafts, or do something with my hands

When I teach other people, I prefer to:
__ (V) Show them
__ (A) Tell them or write it out
__ (K) Demonstrate it and then ask them to do it

When I do something new, I prefer to:
__ (V) Look for demonstration, pictures, or diagrams
__ (A) Look for verbal or written instructions and talk with someone
__ (K) Jump in and try right away, learning as I do it

Add up the total for each category. Which category did you mark most often? Visual, Auditory, Kinetic?

____

____

____

This worksheet only provides a few examples so you can start to think about how you prefer to receive information. Many people prefer to receive information in different ways depending on the type of information. People may simply have several learning styles in their overall learning repertoire. What do you think is your preferred learning style? Do you have more than one preference?

____

____

____

____

____

____

____

____

Meet Alexa

Alexa is from the United States. She lives and works in Bologna, Italy. After graduating from college and earning her Teaching English as a Foreign Language (TEFL) certification, she moved abroad to teach English and to learn Italian. She currently works as an English teacher at a private school in Bologna's city center. Alexa takes Italian classes in the mornings and teaches English in the afternoons and evenings.

Alexa moved to Italy to find work as an English teacher, but went to Bologna specifically because she wanted to fully immerse herself in the Italian language and Italy's culture. In her free time, Alexa travels throughout Italy, taking advantage of the well-organized public transportation system. She also writes articles on her internet blog to help others come to Italy.

The transition was really easy in the beginning! When I first arrived, everything was shiny and new. My life felt like a vacation! It still does to an extent, but over time things got more difficult. The honeymoon phase ended and I started to have thoughts about home. Don't get me wrong, I love living in Italy, but it takes time to adjust to a new culture. For me, the biggest barrier is the language, but every week I am able to communicate a bit better.

I found it really easy to criticize cultural differences in the beginning of my adventure. I often thought to myself, "in America we would never do it that way." It's okay to compare cultures, but it's important to make a strong effort to understand the culture you're in and why people do the things they do.

Alexa

STRATEGY #3: Get connected

The basis for almost all positive cross-cultural adjustment is communication. This includes communicating with a self-awareness of what we are saying and paying attention to the differences between ourselves and the people we are talking to. It requires that we be attentive and listen with all our senses to judge how our message is being received and that we are to receive feedback through direct and indirect signals. This sort of awareness, sensitivity, and readiness helps us know if we are being understood and creates conditions of trust, mutual respect, and openness that foster meaningful interactions, communications, and friendships. Communication also helps us solve problems and emotionally adjust by bringing new information, advice, and support to us from others.

Most of the failures in communication do not occur because we are self-absorbed, lack concern with what is being said or who is saying it, or lack sincerity. Most failures occur because we shift our focus from communicating to reacting. This occurs when someone is talking to us and we become preoccupied with crafting our response in our head, even as they speak. The shift from communicating to reacting often happens because something has occurred that has threatened us in some way or has made us defensive. Feelings of confusion, fear, anger, hurt, insult, danger, risk, or a perceived loss of safety, can all bring about a defensive reaction in our minds and sidetrack healthy communications.

Social contact
We cannot get connected to others if we do not first make contact with them, either directly or indirectly. Fortunately, the explosion of social media on the internet has made making contact both easy and globally available. However, there are many other contexts for making contact while living abroad. Our contact may occur in the

context of local traditions and celebrations, family and friendship ties, beliefs we share in common with others, common experiences, or patterns of daily life and social interaction for business, pleasure, or education. Of course, one of the best ways to strengthen our social contact it to pay attention to and cultivate the social relationships we already have. Sometimes reaching out to others to expand our social connections requires a dedicated effort on our part. This can be especially true if we become depressed during adjustment to our new life abroad and begin to socially withdraw.

> *With social media you can begin before you arrive by connecting with local groups and don't be afraid to ask the veterans of expat life for help.*
>
> *Meghan*

Social isolation

There are often practical and self-imposed limits between the interaction of expatriates and the local culture. The term 'expatriate bubble' is used to describe conditions were expatriates limit their exposure to locals in preference for interacting with other expatriates and who use stores and services that cater to expatriates, as opposed to using those frequented by locals. It is natural that there would be some differences in preferences between expatriates and locals. After all, expatriates are bridging two cultures, their own and the local one, so they may find a balanced mix of interaction is their most comfortable adjustment strategy. The problem arises when we segregate, self-isolate, or limit exposure to local culture in a way that limits our enjoyment of the host nation, restricts their understanding of local culture, or stops personal growth.

To some degree, social isolation may also simply reflect the difficulty of building new relationships abroad. Part of the challenge is that every culture has its own rules and preferences for how they spend their spare time. Some cultures make a sharp division between work life and social life, so they limit the bleed over of work relationships into their social lives. People in different cultures may also socialize in different ways, with different rules guiding interaction between age, status, and gender groups. Difficulty in connecting to locals can result in a smaller social circle and can contribute to a tendency to spend time with other expatriates.

Expatriates the world over are often seen as existing in cosseted bubbles, living and interacting only with those who share their nationality or language. But the reality, like the nature of the expat world itself, is complicated and changing. Nowadays expats (in Singapore) are just as likely to be Asian as they are Western and an increasing number of professionals are moving abroad independently, instead of on a company-sponsored posting.

Kate

Exercise #13
My social connections

List at least three people, groups, or communities that you are
connected with.

____

____

____

____

____

____

____

How can you expand the *number* of your social connections?

____

____

____

____

____

____

____

How can you improve the *quality* of your social connections?

____

____

____

____

____

____

____

STRATEGY #4: Change how you think

How we think shapes how we assess and appraise what we observe and experience. The processes of assessment and appraisal work on two levels. On one hand, they help us understand what we directly observe and experience. This is our direct appraisal. On the other hand, our thoughts also help us anticipate experiences. So, we often already have an expectation formed in our mind of what we will observe or experience before it happens. This is our anticipatory appraisal. The nature of our expectations is shaped, in part, by our own cultural lens. When there is a large difference between our expectations and local reality, we can experience a cognitive disconnect. We may have to stop and rethink about what we are seeing and what it means. We may have to find a new lens for understanding it.

Since how we think is important in shaping how we perceive and react to what is happening around us, it gives us the opportunity to make adjustments that lessen the impact of changes we may be experiencing and make them easier to incorporate into our mental framework. Experiencing new cultures often requires that we reframe how we think. This can be especially important in reframing stressful events. Instead of exclusively focusing on the negative, we can instead try positive reframing, practicing gratitude, or finding new opportunities in the middle of problems. Of course, some events are major catastrophes that can resist positive reframing, but in general we are able to find an alternative way of looking at most challenges and problems. It may be as simple as remembering that a minor problem is just that, a minor problem, and being thankful that we have been spared worse.

One of the elements that drive how we think is how we appraise problems. For example, do we tend exaggerate the scope of a problem when it occurs? This sort of distortion occurs when we anticipate that a problem will cause a dramatically unfavorable outcome without looking more closely first. This type of thinking tends to magnify the bad results that we anticipate. A thought pattern might go like this: If I don't get to my visa appointment, I will not get my visa renewed and I will have to abandon my dream of living abroad. Or, my friend did not call when he said he would. I will never make friends here.

Another element of how we appraise problems is how we attribute their causes. Do we see problems as unique and specific or do we see problems as global in nature, always occurring, and always driven by external forces we cannot control? The key is understanding what we think about our own ability to handle problems and whether we have an instinct to believe that control is either inside or outside of our capabilities. Many times, when we have confidence and perceive that we have some control over our lives, we have a sense of action and responsibility. We might say something like: It will be hard but am sure I can do it. Alternatively, when we place control of problems outside our perceived capabilities, we might feel that external factors, fate, or circumstance are driving the outcome. We might say something like: It is just too hard to be successful because no one will ever give me a chance. The good news is that how we look at things is largely up to us, we can change how we think and, so, change our lives.

Part of changing how we think involves changing how we talk to ourselves. We tend to have an internal narrative and self-image running in the background of our minds. This type of self-talk tends to confirm our self-perception and our view of the world. It also tends to reaffirm how we cope. For example, when delayed by a difficult problem, we might routinely say something positive to ourselves something like: Tomorrow is a new day. It is important for us to be aware of our self-talk and whether it tends to be positive or negative.

My biggest regret is dwelling on what I was missing at home instead of realizing how incredible the experience I was being given was.

Savannah

Exercise #14
Challenging negative thoughts

(Stress, anxiety, poor self-esteem, and depression can be amplified by negative thoughts. Challenging negative thoughts can help us change them.)

Think about a problem you are currently facing or one that you believe you will face soon. What do you think about it? Answer the following questions to assess your thoughts.

Are my thoughts based on emotions or facts?

____

____

____

____

____

Is there evidence for my thoughts?

____

____

____

____

____

Is there evidence that refutes or is contrary to my thoughts?

____

____

____

____

____

Am I attempting to interpret this situation without all the evidence?

What would a friend think about this situation?

Will this problem matter a year from now? How about five years from now?

Exercise #15
Alternative thinking

(How we look at things is a decision we make. We can choose to re-frame the things we see in new ways. By changing our thoughts, we can change our attitude towards something and change the way we feel.)

Think about a problem you are facing. Write down the negative thoughts that come into your mind. When you are finished, take the time to re-frame every negative thought by finding evidence that refutes it and an alternative positive thought. Then write them down. For example, you may feel you will never find a job. The refuting evidence might be your skills and work ethic. The alternative positive thought might be, I will find a job, it will just take some time.

Negative Thought

____

____

____

____

____

____

____

Refuting Evidence

____

____

____

____

____

____

____

____

____

____

____

____

____

____

Meet Jim and Jiab

Married couple Jim and Jiab moved from the United States to retire in Granada, a culturally rich college town in southern Spain. Before retirement Jim was a lawyer–turned–economics teacher and Jiab was a banker and credit risk manager. They considered other places to live such as Costa Rica, but the deciding factor for them was the cost of living in Granada. Yet, Granada also offers many excellent restaurants, festivals, and hundreds of centuries-old buildings, castles and churches. It is also the site of Alhambra, a breathtaking palace with Islamic decor that is designated as a UNESCO World Heritage site. Jiab is originally from Thailand and the couple still enjoys travel. They have traveled locally to Madrid, to Thailand to visit relatives, and return to the United States about twice a year.

Granada has a way of slowing you down [so that] you're more present. Here we walk everywhere, we're in the moment — the lifestyle means we sit outside, we see people.

Jim

We just fell in love with Granada. It's a really international city, I love its size [250,000 people], it's really vibrant, and we can walk or take the bus everywhere.

Jiab

STRATEGY #5: Solve problems

It is a reality that our lives are not free of problems. That is ok since we often enjoy variety in life and its challenges. Dealing with the problems that life brings, both big and small, is simply part of the experience of living fully. We tend to think of solving problems rationally. We identify a problem, task, or goal, gather our resources, and set about charting a path to resolve or attain it. While true, problem-solving also has social and emotional aspects, especially for expatriates. We often need advice or assistance when living abroad and facing problems in a new environment.

There are two types of problems. The first are problems of presence. These usually specific problems such as solving a problem, completing a task, getting something accomplished, or responding to a specific situation. There are also problems of absence. These deal with things that are missing in our lives. When you think about a problem, you can ask yourself, does it involve something that is present now and occurring in your life that you need to resolve? Or, does it involve something this is missing in your life that you need to create, find, or replace?

Know what you want
We can think of problem-solving as completing a path from point A to point B. We are presented a challenge or task and need to complete a series of action to resolve or achieve it. In order to get to a destination, we must first know what it is. Sometimes small problems are nested within larger questions that we must ask ourselves. For example, if you need to find a place to live, you may ask yourself, do I want to live in the city center, near work, by the beach or mountains? What is most important about where I live? Knowing what we want and what is important to us often provides a helpful background and may help prevent some regret over our

decisions later. This example hints at another consideration. Many problems are interconnected in some way. For example, if I were to prioritize living close to work does that make social life, shopping, or recreation easier or more difficult? It helps when we keep the big picture in mind.

Don't make it worse

Part of solving problems is not creating more. There is a human tendency to want to get in the last word in an argument. This can lead to an escalation of problems. Sometimes it is good for us to simply stop, take a break, and regain our perspective when facing a problem. This small break is a good time to seek out emotional support and advice, especially from close friends or others who have been through similar experiences. But we do not want to wait too long before addressing a problem. Problems often get worse the longer we delay addressing them. We must stay proactive and move ahead when faced with challenges, even if our steps forward are small. One way to maintain our forward momentum is to establish a daily routine. Having a daily or weekly routine provides and anchor from which we can explore options. It can provide us an essential sense of stability and security and prevent downslides by staying active and engaged in the world around us.

Problem-solving support

When we connect to others, we get a lot of practical help. This help can include instrumental support. The idea of instrumental support was developed by Richard Lazarus and Susan Folkman and consists of the social support we receive that helps use tackle the practical problems we face. For example, we can receive advice, knowledge, or others might share their experiences and lessons learned with us. The key feature of instrumental support is that it helps us solve a problem or complete a task. Sometimes it can help us think about a problem in a new way or simply provide us a strategy to minimize a problem's effects. Having local or expatriate allies is essential since they have already faced the same problems. A benefit is that when we learn new strategies, we not only cope better but we are more prepared to help others in the future. Sometimes the problems we face are serious, but, when we can, it is always helpful to keep a positive, upbeat, and playful attitude. When we keep a lighthearted attitude, it helps keep our social relationships open.

Oh, and the (Portuguese) bureaucracy can be infuriating. Few people in the government can speak English or explain how things work, and we're regularly given different answers by different people.

Lauren

People like meeting other expats who might have had the same problems and dealt with them. But they also want to meet locals who know the city even better and want to share their culture.

Malte

Exercise #16
Solving problems

*(When problems or stresses begin to overwhelm us, it is often helpful
to break them down into smaller problem-solving steps.)*

Think about a problem you face. Walk through these four problem-
solving steps.

Accept the uncontrollable
What parts of the problem are not in your control?
What are you willing to give up, change, or accept?

____

____

____

____

____

____

____

Focus on the controllable
Even though you may not be able to control all aspects of the
problem, what can you control? What thoughts, feelings, and
behaviors can you control to make the problem more manageable
right now?

____

____

____

____

____

____

____

Look to your strengths

What personal strengths do you and your partner bring to the situation? What are you each good at?

____

____

____

____

____

____

Use your strengths and focus on the positive

Think about your strengths. How can you make the problem better right now? Are there any other positives or opportunities you can take advantage of?

____

____

____

____

____

____

____

Spotlight on culture
Handling conflict

While disagreements and conflict are an inevitable part of life, research has found that there are broad differences in preferred methods for handing conflict across cultures. Gert Hofstede, has extensively compared cultures and provides insight into cultural biases in managing conflict. Here are some of his findings.

United States

The United States has a value system that emphasizes competition, achievement, and success, with success being defined by the winner or best-in-the-field. It is not surprising that studies have found that persons from the United States may have a preference for competing to resolve conflict, but also have a preference for avoiding or compromising.

South Korea

South Koreans strive for consensus and group loyalty and relationships are highly valued. An effective manager in South Korea is a supportive one, and decision-making is achieved through group involvement. Studies have found that South Koreans prefer collaborating, compromising, and accommodating to resolve conflict.

Saudi Arabia

Similar to South Korea, Saudi Arabia is a collectivist society that values close group relationships. However, it is more similar to the United States in handling conflict. There is a preference for decisive managers who emphasize competition and performance, so there may be a preference for resolving conflict by competition or by direct decree. This may be partly due to Saudi Arabia's preference for hierarchical organization, centralized authority, and the obedience of subordinates.

STRATEGY #6: Feel better

In addition to problem-focused coping, researchers have also identified emotion-focused coping as a response to stress. While problem-solving tends to focus outward, emotion-focused coping focuses inward. Cultural shock can create feelings of anxiety, confusion, alienation or loneliness, and powerlessness or helplessness. It is not a surprise that emotion-focused coping helps relieve our feelings of emotional distress.

Emotion-focused coping includes all the things we might do to feel better, such as distracting ourselves temporarily from a problem by watching a movie or engaging in recreation, finding comfort in food or drink, seeking companionship, exercising or being active, meditating or praying, suppressing emotions, or denying the problem. It is easy to see that some of these strategies might lead to trouble. The key is that we use the appropriate strategy for the appropriate length of time. For example, can denial be considered a healthy coping strategy? It can when used appropriately. Denial can be a short-term, protective mechanism. Sometimes we need to set a problem aside to prevent ourselves from being psychologically overwhelmed as we gather our emotional and problem-solving resources so we can be strong enough and prepared enough to tackle it. The problem occurs when denial becomes a long-term strategy and we fail to face the current reality and the consequences of inaction. The same holds true for other strategies such as overeating or the inappropriate use of drugs or alcohol.

Here are a few emotion-focused coping strategies.

Find social support
There are a few ways that social support can help us manage stress. Social support through friends or allies gives us the chance to talk about our problems and get them off our chest. Whether the problem is resolved or not, we tend to feel better when we can talk about it with someone who is supportive. A great value of friends is that they help us laugh when things are bad and help us keep our sense of perspective. Secondly, we often get good advice from our friends or others who have had similar experiences. This is helpful in a practical way since it helps us identify steps we can take. But it is also helpful psychologically. When we sense that we have options available to us our feelings of frustration, entrapment, and loss of control can lessen. We may feel less threatened, more capable, and more confident as we face our problems. Our spirits may be lifted and it may be easier regain our perspective, our sense of agency and power, and for us to reframe problems and the way ahead in more positive terms.

Be active
When we face a problem, we have a tendency to either approach and attempt to resolve the problem or to avoid it. This is known as the fight or flight syndrome. But sometimes we can become overwhelmed and paralyzed into inaction by problems. Sometimes we freeze. This can lead to a stalemate where we may be indecisive and not moving forward. One way to overcome this inertia, and to maintain a sense of motivation and a propensity to act on our problems, is to be active in some way. This can include recreation, hobbies, other interests, or learning a new skill. The key is that we get up, get out, and get going. We also tend to find it gratifying when we create something or when we help others. When we create or give to others it creates inner strength, reaffirms our sense of self-worth, and connects us in a human way to the world around us.

Relax

Although it may be difficult to relax when faced with stress, daily relaxation exercises are a good way to train your mind to stay calm in the face of hardship. There are many options, including breathing exercises, meditation, progressive muscle relaxation, listening to music, or simply enjoying some quiet time by oneself. All of these techniques help us create a state of inner calmness. When we condition our mind and body to stay calm for a few minutes each day, it makes it easier for us bring back a feeling of calmness and relaxation when we under stress.

Make sure you are connected with your faith, whatever religion you are. Being away from home is sad and sometimes difficult, so finding your faithful tribe such as a church community will help you cope with that emotion.

JM

We all know at least one expat who is a Negative Nelly (or Ned). You meet them in expat meet-up groups and trolling around expat forums. You can spot Negative Nelly right away because nothing is ever good enough in her new country – the service is bad; the weather is terrible; the food is too bland or too spicy; nothing works the way it does 'back home'.

Alison

If you are friends with someone living abroad and they go quiet on social media for a while – reach out! They may be struggling, unable to post 'the usual pretty pictures of their life' because, quite frankly, they may not be seeing the 'glamorous' side of their life right now. They may be struggling and feel unable to share it with anyone.

Carole

Exercise #17
Simple meditation

1. Find a comfortable place where you can sit without distractions
   for at least 15 minutes.

2. Sit comfortably with your back upright and without back support,
   if physically possible.

3. Close your eyes and focus within.

4. Focus your attention.

   - You can focus your attention on your breath and breathing.
     Breathe in and out. Just watch the movement of your in and
     out breaths.
   - You can repeat an affirmation (a positive statement about
     yourself and life). If you use an affirmation, try to feel what
     it means to you.
   - You can focus on your heartbeat.
   - You can use any other method with which you feel
     comfortable.

5. If you notice your mind wandering, that's okay, just bring your
   focus back to your technique.

6. When you have completed meditating, it is a good idea to give
   yourself a few minutes to acclimate slowly back into the present.

Exercise #18
Visualizing success

(When we visualize something, we increase our motivation and our confidence that we can do it. Visualization exercises generally fall into two categories. We can visualize a future we want to achieve. Or, we can visualize ourselves doing something to increase our self-confidence. Visualizations expose and help acclimate our minds to new experiences and reduce our mental barriers for actually completing an activity in the future.)

In this exercise you will imagine successfully doing something that you find difficult or are reluctant or afraid to do.

Imagine an activity that you would like to do but are shy or reluctant to do.

____

____

____

____

____

____

Imagine all the details involved in the activity. Be as realistic as possible. Where are you? What people are with you or around you? Are you inside or outside? What are you doing? Imagine each step or action you are doing.

____

____

____

____

____

____

Imagine that you are completing the activity successfully. How do you feel? Are you happy, satisfied, relieved, proud, tired, energized, thankful? What did you do? How are others around you reacting?

____

____

____

____

____

____

When relocating abroad, expatriates face a whole new set of cultural norms, attitudes and behaviors.

Matthew

Remember that life travels at a difference pace in some destinations, so the speed of service or anything else may be at a more relaxed pace. That is okay, just accept it. One final piece of advice, even if you don't agree with the practices or beliefs of the culture you are in, at least you should respect them.

Shane

Spotlight on culture
Respect for elders
Demographics and the age structures of countries are changing around the world. These changes often impact how the elderly are treated, although traditional preferences for respect persist in many countries.

United States
Americans expect their children to be independent. The American workplace can seem ageist to the elderly, as youth culture is celebrated. The older generation can live hundreds of miles away from their children. As in many other countries, the care of the elderly is a social issue.

Philippines
Family relationships and parental authority are valued in the Philippines. Traditionally, when an elder is met one bows slightly and takes the elder's hand and presses to one's forehead. This respectful gesture is called *mano po*.

China
Elders in China are held in great respect and treated as such, both in business and socially. Many families live with several generations under one roof. It is traditional for children to care for their parents as they age and to honor the dead.

South Korea
It is customary in South Korean to have a large celebration to mark a parent's 60th and 70th birthdays. The 60th birthday, or *hwan-gap*, is a time when children celebrate their parents' passage into old age.

STRATEGY #7: Keep the big picture in mind

In order to keep a big picture in mind, we first have to have one. Finding a big picture requires that we look at ourselves honestly and assess who we are and what is important to us. The big picture also requires us to look at where we are in life. As we do this, we often find that the unfolding story of our life becomes clearer to us.

One of the hallmarks of being a functioning adult is to be able to sit back and assess what is important. The reason that this is the characteristic of an adult is that sorting out what is important often requires us to put things in perspective and assess their true value. We may have an impulse to over-value temporary or impermanent things. The challenge is not to deny these things. But, rather, to find out what everything has in common. Perhaps we value happiness, but our sense of true happiness is grounded in having new and exciting experiences. Then, we would embrace short-lived experiences along with a life structured in a way to safely bring them to us. Perhaps we value peace and serenity. Then we might examine and minimize some the discomforts, distractions, or toxic people in our lives and structure our lives to create the peaceful environment that energizes us. The key is for us to be able to look back on our lives with a minimum of self-imposed regret and say to ourselves that our lives were well-spent.

Inner- versus outer-directed
When we are trying to understand the meaning of our lives, it is helpful to reflect on our values. What is the source of the values we hold and the things we seek? One way to think about this is to consider whether we are primarily inner-directed or outer-directed. If we are inner-directed, we might be guided by our own thoughts, values, conscience. An inner-directed person might have a strong sense that they are in control of their lives, not in the sense of being

domineering, but in the sense that they have confidence in their own perspectives and are happy to lead themselves. An outer-directed person may be more tuned in with what is happening around them. They may feel an attraction to feeling that they are a part of a group. They may more strongly appreciate the norms, values, standards, and behaviors of society or their friendship groups. They may feel an attraction to conform with these standards to reinforce their sense of similarity, belonging, or connectedness. Of course, we may hold a combination of values, strongly holding some personal values while feeling comfortable joining in with some group values.

Where are you at in life?
When we live abroad, we will need to adjust to the way of life around us. But this adjustment occurs simultaneously with the natural progression of our own lives. Erik Erikson, a German-American psychologist, developed a theory of psychosocial development. His theory characterized our lives as a set of stages and tasks that occur as we go through life. For example, he proposed that roughly between the ages of 18 and 40 years old, our primary task is to find love and intimacy. This need to define meaningful relationships with others involves a tension between intimacy and isolation that must be resolved. He also proposed that roughly between the ages of 40 and 65 years old, our primary task is to develop the virtue of caring for oneself and others. Developing this virtue requires that we resolve the tension between generativity (i.e., creating, contributing, and connecting) and stagnation. In this stage, we often explore and reconnect to what our lives mean.

Let's try to put this into the context of an expatriate experience. Imagine we were a 20- or 30-something year old expatriate living abroad. Perhaps, we view the expatriate experience as an adventure, a chance to experience new things, and to mingle and connect with others for adventure, romance, and companionship in shared experiences. In terms of Erikson's stages, this is a match to the need in our life at that point to find intimacy. Of course, we might have other goals like gaining work experience, connecting to our cultural heritage, but the backdrop at that stage of life is a fundamental need to find and experience intimacy in our lives. it will naturally shape our lives whether we are at home or abroad. However, where we are living will have a critical effect of our options and the outcomes at whatever stage of life we are at.

Be content

There is an old saying that says, if you would desire a new set of shoes, think about the man who has no feet. It is a bit of a strong statement, but the intent is to remind us to keep things, especially our desires, in perspective. When we focus too much on our desires and the things we do not have, it can lead to unhappiness, disillusionment, and depressed feelings. Practicing contentment sometimes requires us to stop dwelling on the good things we do not have. Fortunately, practicing contentment also means that we celebrate the good things that we do have. When we look at our lives, we often find we have a lot of things to be thankful for, both big and small.

I can't think of anything that excites a greater sense of childlike wonder than to be in a country where you are ignorant of almost everything. Suddenly you are five years old again.

Bill

Now, after having spent nearly 13 years outside the U.S., the term expat has come to signify having a foot in two cultures, two different viewpoints and ways of living. You may be far away from your home country, but it remains fundamentally rooted in who you are and how you make your way in the world.

Tuula

Exercise #19
My legacy

(To leave a good legacy, we have to first lead a good, purposeful, or thoughtful life. Thinking about our legacy is one way to bring what we are doing today more sharply into focus. It also helps us to think about the lasting impact we will have on those around us.)

1. What do you feel is the purpose of your life? Its meaning?

____

____

____

____

____

2. What do you want to accomplish? What is your greatest struggle?

____

____

____

____

____

3. What kind of a legacy do you want to leave behind when you are gone?

____

____

____

____

____

4. When will feel that you have lived a full life? What must happen?

____

____

____

____

____

____

STRATEGY #8: Define your story

We all have a self-image of who we are in our minds. This image is either conscious of subconscious. This image can do several things. On one hand, it can confirm to us who we believe we are right now. On the other hand, it can serve as a guide to who we want to be or how we want to be seen by others. It this sense, it is a role we are fulfilling as we live our lives each day. However, this role is culturally informed. Let's image that you see yourself as a teacher or a musician. As you have grown up you have learned what a teacher or a musician is and what they do. This image is shared with everyone else in your cultural group. You likely have common perceptions about teachers and musicians and these perceptions come with expectations of how teachers and musicians look and act.

The powerful part of all of this is that we get to choose who we are, who we want to be, and how we influence how others see us. We have the freedom to make a personal choice. This choice then, serves as our guide and defines us as we grow, mature, and achieve our destinies. The questions then arise, who are you and who do you want to become? What will be the story of your life? Maybe we do want to be a teacher. It is where we find happiness, a sense of connection, and a sense of giving to others. Maybe we do not want any of the available roles. So, we chart or own path, choosing to become an adventurer or a rebel who cherishes personal freedom as a form of self-expression. Even nonconformity has an image and a story. Whatever image or story we choose to create, we will carry it with us through our expatriate experience. In fact, we will carry it with us through all of life's glories and challenges.

Joseph Campbell was a professor of literature who spent his life studying mythology. After widely reading myths from many cultures and religions, he discovered that myths have common structures and common themes. Roughly, they often involved the journey of a hero or heroine going away from their home to a special world where they complete a great ordeal to capture a prize that redefines who they are. They return home to share the prize. Throughout the journey the hero encounters many challenges, many types of people who are either helpful, deceitful, or threatening, and learns a great deal about themselves.

Like the journey of Joseph Campbell's heroes, we too are on a hero's journey in our own lives. There are a lot of similarities to the expatriate experience, which also involves a departure from home, experiencing many trials, encountering many different sorts of helpful and unhelpful people, and learning about ourselves in new, surprising, and profound ways.

So, we can ask ourselves, what is our image of who are we, what do we want to become, and where are we on our personal journey of exploring life through adventure and trials? These are all elements of our life's story. However, our life is an unfolding story. What character are we? Where are we at in our adventure? How do we want to be remembered when our adventure ends? The good news is that our story is not over and we have the opportunity to both redefine ourselves and to navigate life's challenges in ways that are uplifting, personally meaningful, create a life story that proudly captures who we really are, and give us the opportunity to connect and share with others.

> *I moved to Amsterdam to escape a failed relationship; a broken heart without job, house or love that had to re-define itself through a new challenge. Moving abroad was a risk and a necessity.*
>
> *Agnese*

Exercise #20
The hero's/heroine's journey

(In this exercise you will follow your life's path as an expatriate journey.)

The Beginning – My world
Describe your world before moving abroad. What did you do, how did you feel, what did you want?

____

____

____

____

____

The Call to Adventure
What made you feel the need to change your life? What were you reaching for? How did you imagine life abroad would be?

____

____

____

____

____

Crossing the Threshold
Describe your move abroad. How did it feel to leave your home behind? How did it feel to arrive in a new country? What were your emotions?

____

____

____

____

____

____

____

Tests, Allies, and Enemies

When we arrive at a new country, we encounter many challenges.
Sometimes we are helped by new friends and allies. Sometimes
others may try to take advantage of us or lead us astray. Describe the
challenges and people you have met in your new country. Who or
what has been helpful? Who or what has not been helpful or has
tempted you? What trials or challenges have you overcome?

____

____

____

____

____

Learning About Myself

When we have a major change in our lives, we often learn a lot about
ourselves. What major challenges have you overcome? What new
strengths did you discover? Is living abroad different from what you
thought it would be? What have you learned about yourself? Has
your perspective on living abroad changed? How has your view of
yourself changed?

____

____

____

____

____

____

____

What Can I Give to Others?

When we overcome a major challenge in life, we often learn new, deep, and important insights. We are often more prepared to help others, provide them advice, or guide them. How has your view of yourself as an expatriate changed? What new knowledge, skills, and insights have you gained that you can share with others? What gift does your expatriate experience give to you personally?

____

____

____

____

____

____

____

SCENARIOS

Read the following scenarios. What influences do you think are shaping each expatriate experience?

Learning in Lisbon

Kay has always wanted to travel. She has decided to start a career teaching English abroad. She is attending a 30-day Teaching English as a Foreign Language (TEFL) course in Lisbon, Portugal. She believes this will give her the teaching skills and cross-cultural experience she needs to live abroad. She is excited to be in Lisbon and enjoys exploring the city with the other foreign students. The teacher connects the students with Portuguese students who want to improve their English language skills and they often do activities together such a dining out or sightseeing.

What type of expatriate is Kay (worker, retiree, student, adventurer, romantic, etc.)?

____

____

What stage of cultural adjustment is Kay at (honeymoon, shock, adjustment, integration)? Why do you believe so?

____

____

____

____

____

____

What can Kay do to prepare for her first teaching assignment
abroad?

____

____

____

____

____

Frustrated in Vietnam

John is retired and has been living in Vietnam for about 4 months. His initial excitement about living abroad is starting to fade. He is increasingly frustrated with the hot tropical climate, the limited availability of his favorite Western foods, and the difficulty in getting around in the heavy urban traffic. He moved abroad to have an exciting life on a limited income but is finding that he has little to do during the day. John has a restless feeling each day and is not sure he made the right choice. He spends most evenings socializing with other expatriates at bars and finds himself complaining more and more about the local people and daily life.

What type of expatriate is John (worker, retiree, student, adventurer, romantic, etc.)?

____

____

What stage of cultural adjustment is John at (honeymoon, shock, adjustment, integration)? Why do you believe so?

____

____

____

____

Do you think John is making healthy coping choices?

____

____

____

____

How can John improve the quality of his life?

____

____

____

____

Getting along in Mexico

Sam has been living in Mexico for almost a year since retiring there to enjoy the warm weather and improve his health. After many ups and downs, he finally feels comfortable. He has a settled weekly routine that includes a morning walk, time spent on the internet chatting with friends back home, and fishing in the afternoon. He attends a church close by and helps with small volunteer projects there. He has connected with several other expatriate groups in the area and meets with them to watch soccer games on the television. His language skills have improved enough that he is able to make new local friends and have conversations with his existing friends in their language. Sam is aware that he does not know everything but he believes that he understands the challenges in Mexico better than before and is increasingly confident that he can manage them.

What type of expatriate is Sam (worker, retiree, student, adventurer, romantic, etc.)?

____

____

What stage of cultural adjustment is Sam at (honeymoon, shock, adjustment, integration)? Why do you believe so?

____

____

____

____

What healthy coping and adjustment choices has Sam made?

____

____

____

____

Jerry in Japan

Jerry is a retiree living in Japan. He has lived there for over twenty years and previously owned a small business there. His wife is Japanese. He is fluent in speaking and writing Japanese. He often helps other expatriates find housing, register their cars, and navigate through the local city government for other things they need. Jerry does some translating on the side to help others but it is just a hobby. He likes to help expatriates who own businesses in the area and enjoys singing karaoke with his expatriate and Japanese friends.

What type of expatriate is Jerry (worker, retiree, student, adventurer, romantic, etc.)?

____

____

What stage of cultural adjustment is Jerry at (honeymoon, shock, adjustment, integration)? Why do you believe so?

____

____

____

____

____

What healthy coping and adjustment choices has Jerry made?

____

____

____

____

____

CONCLUSION

The topic of how to cope and adjustment while living abroad is immensely broad. It covers elements of counseling, sociology, and psychology. The goal of this book was to condense some of the relevant ideas about coping and present them in the context of the expatriate experience. While many ideas can be broadly applied across our lives, the experience of living abroad has many unique elements that make it worth examining separately. The exercises in this book were designed to help you work through your own journey of self-exploration. I hope you found this book worthwhile and valuable.

Postscript

As this book was being written, the world was still in the midst of the COVID-19 pandemic. The coronavirus pandemic has had an unprecedented impact on the world. Many countries have implemented travel restrictions, enacted mandatory quarantines, closed borders, restricted air, land, and sea points of entry, and prohibited non-citizens from entry. Some countries are encouraging expatriates to leave and return home. Some countries are appealing for expatriates to return due to concerns that conditions abroad might be unsafe or unmanageable for their citizens due to unpredictable changes in medical or bureaucratic conditions.

The impact that the pandemic will have on the global expatriate community is still unknown. Many countries and cities are financially dependent on the flow of tourists and expatriates. The economic impact of travel restrictions on tourist enclaves and expatriate communities may put their survival at risk and reshape them in new ways. It is not yet known how expatriate challenges and opportunities will be impacted by these changes, although it is a certainty that they will be in some way.

BIBLIOGRAPHY

Ackerman, Courtney E. (2020, April 17). *What is self-efficacy theory in psychology?* Positive Psychology. https://positivepsychology.com/self-efficacy/

American expat living in Italy – Interview with Alexa. (2020, January 29). Expats Blog. https://www.expatsblog.com/articles/1977/american-expat-living-in-italy-interview-with-alexa

American expat living in Spain – Interview with Jiab and Jim. (2019, October 30). Expats Blog. https://www.expatsblog.com/articles/1979/american-expat-living-in-spain-interview-with-jiab--jim

Art, Antoine. (2020, February 26). *The life of a serial expat.* https://www.antoineart.com/artist-blog/the-life-of-a-serial-expat

Beating negativity – Our tips for a positive life abroad. (2012, October 23). CheeseWeb. https://cheeseweb.eu/2012/10/beating-expat-negativity-power-positive-thinking/

Bhaskar-Shrinivas, Purnima; Harrison, David A.; Shaffer, Margaret A.; and Luk, Dora M. (2004). Academy of Management. *What we have learned about expatriate adjustment? Answers accumulated from 25 years of research.* https://journals.aom.org/doi/pdf/10.5465/ambpp.2004.13863144

Bryant, Sue. (2019, July 17). *10 cultural differences between China and the US.* Country Navigator. https://countrynavigator.com/blog/global-talent/cultural-differences-us-vs-china/

Chowdhury, Madhuleena. (2020, June 8). *What is coping theory?* Positive Psychology. https://positivepsychology.com/coping-theory/

Digital life for the Expat Wife – Interview with Tal. (2015, May 14). http://www.expatsinbiz.com/digital-life-for-the-expat-wife-interview-with-tal/

Expat Child. https://expatchild.com/category/expat-life-articles/expat-personal-stories/expat-interviews/

Expat Interview. http://www.expatsinbiz.com/expat-interviews/

Expatriates. I research net. http://psychology.iresearchnet.com/industrial-organizational-psychology/recruitment/expatriates/

Filipino expat living in United Arab Emirates – Interview with JM Kayne. (2020, January 17). Expats Blog. https://www.expatsblog.com/articles/1975/filipino-expat-living-in-united-arab-emirates-interview-with-jm-kayne

Goldberg, Shawn. *Self-care toolkit.* https://socialworkmanager.org/wp-content/uploads/2017/10/Selfcare-toolkit.pdf

Hill, Catey. (2019, August 10). *How this couple retired to Spain's gorgeous Andalusia region on about $40,000 a year — and you can, too.* Market Watch. https://www.marketwatch.com/story/how-this-couple-retired-to-the-gorgeous-spanish-countryside-for-about-40000-a-year-and-you-can-too-2019-05-14

Holland, Jason. (2019, December 2). *What is an Expat?* International Living. https://internationalliving.com/what-is-an-expat-qa/

Hofstede, Geert. Hofstede Insights. https://www.hofstede-insights.com/

Interview with: Maximilian Wolff - A German expat in living in Poland. Europe language jobs blog. https://www.europelanguagejobs.com/index.php/blog/interview-maximillian-wolff-german-expat-poland

Japanese greetings. https://www.japan-guide.com/e/e2000.html

Kakade, Manasi. *Decode a culture – Perception of Time (Monochroic vs. Polychronic)*. https://manasikakade.com/blog/2015/05/decode-a-culture-perception-of-time-monochronic-vs-polychronic/

Karsten, Matthew. (2019, October 23). *Why I quit being a digital nomad*. https://expertvagabond.com/quit-digital-nomad-life/

Kim, Jihyun and Meyers, Renee A. (2012, August). *Cultural Differences in Conflict Management Styles in East and West Organizations*. Journal of Intercultural Communication, 29, 1404-1634. https://immi.se/intercultural/nr29/kim.html

Kim, Sean. (2020, July 31). *There are 12 types of expats out there. Which one are you?* Rype. https://www.rypeapp.com/blog/types-of-expats/

Lauren After 70 countries, why I moved to Lisbon, Portugal. (2020, July 8). https://www.neverendingfootsteps.com/why-i-moved-to-lisbon-portugal

Lipowski, Jessica. (2015, May 6). *Culture with travel: Interview with #culturetrav founder Nicolette Orlemans*. https://jessicalipowski.com/nicolette-orlemans-cultural-reflections/

Lipowski, Jessica. (2015, April 28). *Expat life: Tips to integrate in a new culture*. https://jessicalipowski.com/expat-life/

Lipowski, Jessica. (2015, May 19). *The road less traveled: Interview with #TRLT co-founder Savannah Grace*. https://jessicalipowski.com/trlt-savannah-grace/

Lipowski, Jessica. (2015, October 13). *The road less travelled: Interview #TRLT co-founder Shane Dallas*. https://jessicalipowski.com/trlt-shane-dallas/

Lisitsa, Ellie. (2014, January 4). *Weekend Homework Assignment: Self Care (Who Am I?).* The Gottman Institute. .https://www.gottman.com/blog/weekend-homework-assignment-self-care-who-am-i/

Maclachlan, Matthew. (2016, November 9). *The best (and worst) things about an expat assignment.* Communicaid. https://www.communicaid.com/cross-cultural-training/blog/living-and-working-abroad-the-expatriate-experience/

Mayberry, Kate. (2017, March 17). *Why do expats live in bubbles?* BBC. https://www.bbc.com/worklife/article/20170308-why-do-expats-live-in-bubbles

McLeod, Saul. (2018). *Erik Erikson's staged of psychosocial development.* Simple Psychology. https://www.simplypsychology.org/Erik-Erikson.html

McMahon, John. (2019, January 1). *Semi-retired and living a full life in Bangkok.* International Living. https://internationalliving.com/semi-retired-and-living-a-full-life-in-bangkok-mag-2019-1/

Meditation for beginners. Synchronicity Foundation. https://synchronicity.org/meditation-for-beginners?gclid=EAIaIQobChMIhqr-kInu6gIVGInICh1l2QMnEAAYASAAEgIllvD_BwE#How-do-you-meditate

Migration and migrant population statistics. Eurostat. https://ec.europa.eu/eurostat/statistics-explained/index.php/Migration_and_migrant_population_statistics#:~:text=2.4%20million%20immigrants%20entered%20the,non%2DEU%2D27%20citizens.

Migration Data Portal. (2020, June 9). International Students.
https://migrationdataportal.org/themes/international-
students#:~:text=In%202017%2C%20there%20were%20over,Germany%2
0and%20the%20Russian%20Federation.

Mobbs, Carole H. (2019, October 2). *Expats and Mental Health*. Expat
Child. https://expatchild.com/expats-and-mental-
health/#:~:text=Data%20from%20The%20Mental%20Health,and%20depre
ssion%20after%20the%20move.

My humble words of wisdom to future expats. (2014, March 3).
https://www.theaccidentalaustralian.com/my-humble-words-of-wisdom-to-
future-expats/

Osten, Caren. (2016, October 5). *Are you really listening – Or just waiting
to talk?* Psychology Today. https://www.psychologytoday.com/us/blog/the-
right-balance/201610/are-you-really-listening-or-just-waiting-talk

Overcoming culture shock in Thailand. (2014, May 18). Tieland to
Thailand. https://www.tielandtothailand.com/overcoming-culture-shock-
thailand/

Personal Space – China doesn't have it. China Change.
https://chinachange.org/2011/03/11/personal-space-china-doesnt-have-it/

Pofeldt, Elaine. (2018, August 20). *Digital Nomadism Goes Mainstream.*
Forbes. https://www.forbes.com/sites/elainepofeldt/2018/08/30/digital-
nomadism-goes-mainstream/#4d61a12b4553

Pogosyan, Marianna. (2020, May 27). *Reframe stress.* Psychology Today.
https://www.psychologytoday.com/us/blog/between-
cultures/202005/reframe-stress

PWC's 2019 Annual Corporate Directors Survey. PWC.
https://www.pwc.com/us/en/services/governance-insights-
center/library/annual-corporate-directors-survey.html

Roda, Agnese. (2010, December). *Interview with an expat – Myself.* I am expat. https://www.iamexpat.nl/lifestyle/lifestyle-news/interview-expat-myself

Russian etiquette and values. (2020, May 4). Expatica. https://www.expatica.com/ru/living/integration/russian-etiquette-106460/

Saudi Arabian culture. Cultural Atlas. https://culturalatlas.sbs.com.au/saudi-arabian-culture/saudi-arabian-culture-greetings

Stanislawski, Krzysztof. (2019, April 16). *The coping circumplex model: An integrative model of the structure of coping with stress.* Frontiers in Psychology, 10: 694. https://www.ncbi.nlm.nih.gov/pmc/articles/PMC6476932/

State Department Estimates, Citizenship Renunciation, and US Expats: How many Americans live abroad? (2019, November 18). https://www.greenbacktaxservices.com/blog/estimates-show-increase-expats-worldwide/

Stetson University. *Learning style questionnaire.* https://www.stetson.edu/administration/academic-success/media/Learning%20Style%20Questionnaire.docx

Stroeken, Margot. (2018, November 20). *15 quotes on expat life and living abroad.* Expat Energy. https://expat-energy.com/15-expat-quote-expat-life-living-abroad/

The irony of expat life: Pros and Cons. (2019, December 6). https://www.theprofessionalhobo.com/the-irony-of-expat-life-pros-and-cons/

The vicarious trauma toolkit. Office of Victims of Crime. https://ovc.ojp.gov/program/vtt/what-is-vicarious-trauma

Tiwari, Vineeta. *Cultural awareness is crucial for expats.*
https://www.urbanbound.com/blog/cultural-awareness-is-crucial-for-expats

UC Berkley. *Cultural adjustment.*
https://internationaloffice.berkeley.edu/living/cultural.

United Nations. (2019, September 17). *The number of international migrants reaches 272 million, continuing an upward trend in all world regions, says UN.*
https://www.un.org/development/desa/en/news/population/international-migrant-stock-2019.html#:~:text=The%20number%20of%20international%20migrants%20globally%20reached%20an%20estimated%20272,by%20the%20United%20Nations%20today.

Volger, Christopher. *Myth and Movies.*
https://www.tlu.ee/~rajaleid/montaazh/Hero%27s%20Journey%20Arch.pdf

World Values Survey. *Findings and Insights: Live Cultural Map – WVS (1981 – 2015).*
http://www.worldvaluessurvey.org/WVSContents.jsp?CMSID=Findings